Mastering Sambo for Mixed Martial Arts

MASTERING SAMBO
for Mixed
Martial Arts

Scott Sonnon

Paladin Press - Boulder, Colorado

Mastering Sambo for Mixed Martial Arts
by Scott Sonnon

Copyright © 2008 by Scott Sonnon

ISBN 13: 978-1-58160-686-7
Printed in the United States of America

Published by Paladin Press, a division of
Paladin Enterprises, Inc.
Gunbarrel Tech Center
7077 Winchester Circle
Boulder, Colorado 80301 USA
+1.303.443.7250

Direct inquiries and/or orders to the above address.

Visit our website at www.paladin-press.com

Table of Contents

Acknowledgments

I stand on the broad shoulders of men much greater than myself. Every ounce of creativity, every fresh idea and innovative approach, and each new (re)discovery are only the culmination of many generations of coaching, now manifested in this book.

Without those broad shoulders that have lifted me up, carried me, and allowed me to peek at the greatness of their lofty heights, I would be nothing.

So numerous are the names of athletes and coaches who have contributed to writing this book that I am embarrassed to not record them all. So, I thank each of you for giving me the opportunities to learn what I have, organize my thoughts into, hopefully, an intelligent manner, and share them so that others may benefit from our experiences.

I must honor my most significant coaches, Andrew Bachman and Alexander Retuinskih. I must also honor my past teammates, as well as my present: Brandon Jones, Ryan Murdock, Ryan Hurst, and, of course, Joseph Wilson—who agreed to painfully appear in this book. I must honor my business partner, Nikolay Travkin, for without his aid, I could not have spent the last 10 years absorbed in the laboratory of my grappling mat, tinkering. I must honor my close confidant Michael Gannon, for helping me laugh at myself, and remembering that this is only a mad, mad, mad game. Finally, I must honor my wife, Jodie, for tolerating my eccentricities, supporting my long absences, and suffering my obstreperous recovery from injuries. Martial art is truly a living irony: a warrior discipline where peacefulness is learned through fighting.

I am, because we are.

Introduction

If you don't give a damn about martial arts history or how this book came to be written, and all you want is to play with the new game of lower-half submission fighting, I'm not offended. Just skip ahead and start practicing the techniques.

But you must practice them. Even though they look easy to apply, unless you internalize them within a field of competitive resistance, they won't be of any use to you. You won't even see them coming, just because you read about them in this book.

You don't necessarily need to know the history or even the theory of Sambo. Like Pattabhi Jois, the founder of *Asthanga* style, said about yoga, it's "99 percent perspiration and 1 percent theory." Just practice what's in these pages, and eventually you'll get it.

However, one day, you may change your mind and want to know more about why what you're now doing came about and the long, fascinating lineage that you are now part of as a student of RMAX Sambo (RMAX stands for "Surpassing ouRMAXimum Together"). You may also want to understand the history so that you don't repeat the mistakes others have made, and prevent yourself from lengthening your journey and slowing down the evolution of this martial art.

I'd like to welcome you and thank you for studying this book. You're the future, and you will go farther than we have. My only dream is to see as much of that continued evolution as I can before I die.

Why should I, an American, write this book about a Russian discipline? That question deserves an answer. I was the multiple-time USA National Sambo Team Coach, a Grand National and International Sambo Champion, an International Category Sambo Referee (actually one of the more challenging accomplishments considering the written and performance examinations and time required actually officiating matches), and recipient of the coveted "Distinguished Masters of Sport in Sambo"—the highest athletic distinction one could earn in the former USSR.

I also served as the Combat Sambo Chairman for the American Sambo Federation and the Chairman of the International Combat Sambo Commission for FIAS (the world governing body for sambo). In the early years of American Combat Sambo, I was asked to design the first U.S. educational curriculum for combat sambo, which was implemented by more than a hundred schools, universities, and gyms nationwide.

As an international athlete, coach, and referee, I saw the discipline in three dimensions. And as a foreigner who had the privilege of living within the culture, I had the unique opportunity to note the history of theoretical evolution and the technical de-evolution from a objective perspective. Most important, it's given me the opportunity to detach from any cultural tradition or political obligations and continue evolving sambo in the direction I believe appropriate to my fighters.

CHAPTER 1

SAMBO'S EVOLUTION

This history of sambo matches the Winston Churchill description of Russia as a "riddle, wrapped in a mystery, inside an enigma." I spent well over a decade researching, traveling, and studying the many layers that is sambo. What you read of this history may not be the ultimate truth, but it is the most sensible collection of convincing lies that no one to date has been able to accurately debunk.

Only a decade ago, no information could be located anywhere. The younger generations didn't live through the "Cold War" and the phenomenon of clandestine subterfuge that it had institutionalized. I hope to fill that void by sharing my version of the story.

Sambo (Russian: *самбо* but also called Sombo in the United States and sometimes written as SOMBO) is a modern martial art, combat sport, and self-defense system developed in the former Soviet Union, and recognized as an official sport by the USSR All-Union Sports Committee in 1938, presented by Anatoly Kharlampiev.

The word *cambo* is an acronym of *САМозащита Без Оружия* (*SAMozashchita Bez Oruzhiya*), meaning "self-defense without a weapon" in Russian. Sambo has its roots in traditional folk styles of wrestling such as Armenian *Koch*, Georgian *Chidaoba*, Moldovan *Trîntă*, Uzbeki *Kurash*, and Mongolian *Khapsagay*, martial traditions of the West and the Far East.

THE THREE PATRIARCHS OF SAMBO: OSHCHEPKOV, SPIRIDONOV, AND KHARLAMPIEV

The founders of sambo sifted deliberately through all the world's martial arts available to them to augment their military's hand-to-hand combat system. Their distinct concentration, unique perspectives, and individual discoveries resulted in three divergent flavors of sambo.

The primary founder was Vasili Oshchepkov, a Russian, who at the age of 19 was admitted into Japan's Kodokan by Professor Jigoro Kano in 1911. In 1913, Oshchepkov was the first Russian and fourth European in history to receive a black belt ranking in judo (eventually earning his *nidan*, or second-degree black belt, in 1917 out of then only five degrees). In 1921, Oshchepkov served in the Red Army as a commander traveling covertly for special purpose missions into China, where he studied wushu.

Oshchepkov had observed Kano's distillation of Tenjin Shin'yo Ryu jiujitsu and Kito Ryu jiujitsu into what he named judo. Oshchepkov recognized Kano's genius in distilling jiujitsu into a deliberate, educational process. When he returned to Russia, he taught judo to elite Red Army forces at the Central Red Army House. He used Kano's philosophy in formulating the early development of his new Russian art, sambo.

Sambo was in part born of native Russian and other regional styles of grappling and combative wrestling, bolstered with the most useful and adaptable concepts and techniques from the rest of the world. Its early development stemmed from the independent efforts of another Russian, Victor Spiridonov, a combat veteran of World War I, who integrated the techniques of jiujitsu into native wrestling styles. His "soft style" was based on the fact that he received a bayonet wound during the Russo-Japanese war that left his left arm lame.

In 1918, Lenin created *Vseobuch* (*Vseobshchee voennoye obuchienie,* or "General Military Training") under the leadership of N.I. Podvoyskiy to train the Red Army. The task of developing and organizing Russian military hand-to-hand combat training fell to K. Voroshilov, who in turn, created the NKVD physical training center, "Dinamo."

Spiridonov was one of the first grappling and self-defense instructors hired for Dinamo. As a "combatives investigator" for Dinamo, he drew from judo and jiujitsu, Greco-Roman wrestling, American catch wrestling, nonsport British pugilism and Dutch silat, and many Slavic wrestling styles.

Both Oshchepkov and Spiridonov hoped that the Russian styles could be improved by infusing the techniques distilled from jiujitsu by Kano into the new "judo" style of grappling. However, the two were rivals, having differing viewpoints and goals. Spiridonov had envisioned integrating the entire world's fighting systems into one comprehensive style that could adapt to any threat. Oshchepkov focused on creating a consistently successful competitive fighting format for teaching the various departments within the Soviet military.

Students of Oshchepkov, Anatoly Kharlampiev, and Ivan Vasilievich Vasiliev, also traveled the globe to study the native fighting arts of the world. Ten years in the making, their catalog of techniques was instrumental in formulating the early framework of the art eventually referred to as sambo. Oshchepkov's and Spiridonov's independent refinements of Russian fighting skill were inserted into the military's hand-to-hand-combat system.

Kharlampiev is often called the father of sambo. This may be largely semantics since only he had the longevity and political connections to remain with the art while the new system was called sambo. However, Kharlampiev's political maneuvering is single-handedly responsible for the USSR Committee of Sport accepting sambo as the official combat sport of the Soviet Union in 1938—decidedly the "birth" of sambo.

Spiridonov, however, was the first to actually begin referring to the new system as *Samoz,* short for *Samozashchita* or self-defense. Samoz was a softer, more aikido-like system that could be used by smaller, weaker practitioners or even wounded soldiers and secret agents. Spiridonov's inspiration to develop Samoz stemmed from the arm injury he suffered that greatly restricted his ability to practice competitive sambo. Refined versions of sambo are still used today or fused with specific sambo applications to meet the needs of modern Russian commandos.

Each technique for sambo was carefully dissected and considered for its merits, and, if found acceptable in unarmed combat, refined to reach sambo's ultimate goal: stop an armed or unarmed adversary in the least time possible. Thus, the best techniques of jiujitsu and its more competitive cousin judo entered into the sambo repertoire. When the techniques were perfected, they were woven into sambo applications for personal self-defense, as well as for police, crowd control, border guards, secret police, dignitary protection, psychiatric hospital staff, the military, and commandos.

In 1929, Oshchepkov was invited to Dinamo, where he took the sportive form of SAMOZ, coupled with the *Randori* (the competitive act of applying techniques against fully resistant, noncompliant, uncooperative partners, who were attempting to equally apply techniques) concept of judo and the physical education conditioning of wushu, in order to form sambo.

Oshchepkov was enamored with the principle of force-on-force training with a fully resistant partner to experience timing and rhythm to apply techniques. He regularly conducted competitions between Leningrad and Moscow gyms to field-test his theories and techniques. Oshchepkov's study of physical training, early kinesiology, and biomechanics, from such pioneers as Muller, Buk, and Suren was just as important a contribution as the Randori methodology of training techniques under resistance.

The Leningrad Sport Committee abolished Oshchepkov's competition between Leningrad and Moscow fighters. The Soviet regime did not want to recognize the part Japanese judo played in the new free-style fighting (not yet officially named sambo). The government insisted on eliminating every reference to judo. Oshchepkov sent harshly critical letters to the All-USSR Sport Committee, Army's Inspection of Physical Culture and Sport, in Moscow, Leningrad, Ukraine, and Beyond-Caucasus Institutes of Physical Culture.

In 1937, the entire country was under the pressure of nightly arrests. The slogan "better to arrest 10 innocent than to miss one spy" was the basis for the inner security service of that year. The criterion of criminal unreliability was very simple: a man would be arrested if he traveled outside the country or had relatives or friends in other countries. As Oshchepkov had lived in Japan and studied directly with Kano, he belonged to this category. On September 29, 1937, the government decree read: "Oshchepkov Vasili Sergeevich is sufficiently unmasked as Japanese spy . . . citizen Oshchepkov is prose-cuted due to clause 58 article 6." On the night of October 1, 1937, he was arrested in his home. Although he was a staunch patriot wrongly accused of being a Japanese spy, 10 days after his arrest, Oshchepkov was led to a Siberian gulag and subsequently shot in the head for his fraternization with "Japanese imperialists."

Sambo would have disappeared at this point if it weren't for the political savvy of one of Oshchepkov's students, Anatoly Kharlampiev, who used cunning diplomacy to revise sambo. Kharlampiev redefined sambo into a compilation of techniques from various Soviet Republics, an exclusively Soviet state-centric combat system and sport.

In 1938, Kharlampiev's sambo's history was acknowledged, unsurprisingly by the All-USSR State Sport Committee, as his creation based on Soviet training methodologies and heritage. From this point forward, sambo would be known as the fighting art of the motherland. Its adherents and promoters surrounded it with all the patriotic nationalism associated with the former Soviet Union.

In 1942, a covert special military operations school prepared professional assassins named *Volkodav* (wolf killer). The 18 trainers at the school were under the management of two-time Hero of the Soviet Union and Captain of Marine Reconnaissance Nikolai Leonov, a sworn enemy of Adolf Hitler. The training was informally called "a system of survival in extreme conditions" (sometimes just "the system" or *Systema,* and sometimes just "survival" or *Vyzhivaniya).* It was intended strictly for the officers of Soviet Army GRU Spetsnaz, GRU being the country's largest intelligence agency.

One of the best graduates of this school was Alexsei Kadochnikov, often referred to as "Grandfather" and a legend among Soviet Spetsnaz. With direct schooling from the Spiridonov's soft-style tradition, Kadochnikov inserted his academic engineering into this biomechanical perspective on sambo. He established the principle of efficiency as the primary emphasis of all training.

In the 1970s, sambo flooded the international judo competitive scene and revamped the entire perspective of what it meant to grapple. So strong and successful were the Soviet sambists in judo competition that rules changes were made to limit the use of their unique strengths and skills.

In 1980, sambo was a demonstration sport at the Olympic Games in Moscow, Russia. However, due to boycotts of the Olympics, sambo failed to bring sufficient numbers for continued inclusion as a participatory game. That was nearly the death knell for the discipline, as in less than 15 years, the Soviet Union would fall, and with it all of the state-sponsored athletic programs, including sambo.

According to the International Federation of Associated Wrestling Styles (FILA), sambo is one of the four main forms of amateur competitive wrestling practiced internationally today, the others being Greco-Roman wrestling, freestyle wrestling, and judo. FILA accepted sambo as the third style of international wrestling in 1968 until it formed its own organization, the Federation International Amateur Sambo (FIAS), in 1985.

In the mid-1980s, combat sambo competitions began to be held. These no-holds-barred mixed martial art (MMA) competitions invited any fighter of any background to compete in their win by knockout or submission-only competition. Although they were called barbaric, these competitions ushered new life into sambo.

CHAPTER 2

MY ENTRY INTO THE SAMBO TIMELINE

In 1991, I began training with Andrew Bachman, sambo world bronze medalist. With him, I fought on the USA SOMBO Team and was elected as USA National SOMBO Team Coach for the United States SOMBO Association.

Andy introduced me to his coach, who happened to be a U.S. Olympic Greco-Roman wrestler alternate, five-time world sambo silver medalist, a Class A gymnast, and the only man to ever defeat Havalia Hussein (known as "The Great One" in sambo). He received his Master of Sport rank directly from Evgeny Mikhailovich Chumakov, the training partner and advisor to Anatoly Kharlampiev. Chumakov, the USSR champion of sambo, was the author of the famous "100 Lessons of Sambo." Unfortunately, despite this man's incredible fighting abilities, he is now a convicted criminal, and I don't want to give him any energy by publishing his real name.

During this time, I was introduced to Josh Henson, one of the most significant figures in sambo's history, president of FIAS, and international promoter of the sport. Henson and I worked together for quite a few years, and although we had a rocky relationship, I learned a great deal from him.

In 1992, I was appointed as president of the association in charge of American Combat SOMBO. I was appointed with the task of creating the American SOMBO Belt Ranking System. I became very well acquainted with Kharlampiev's sambo through this experience, but my quest demanded that I look deeper into the history. Inconsistencies and blatant disinformation caused me to push further. My investigations caused me to be named "unpatriotic" for studying with Russians and former Soviet coaches and athletes. I became the "black sheep" of American SOMBO for many years, until I basically outlived the involvement of those incumbent officials.

In 1993, I began working with Michael Galperin, whose teacher was one of Oshchepkov's students and Kharlampiev's partners, Ivan Vasiliev. Galperin honored me with as an honorary lifetime member of his organization, the United States Combat Sambo Association. From Galperin, I came to learn more about Oshchepkov's sambo and its distinction from the Kharlampievan style. Those discoveries spurred me deeper into my studies, especially when I stood right in the middle of a huge political eruption in sambo.

In 1993, FIAS split into two organizations. I was still too young in sambo to understand what had happened and why it was so monumental. To me, it just seemed like an argument, a vote, with people storming out of the meeting. The content, the controversy, is irrelevant. It's arguable that all martial arts that get to the level of popularity of sambo will face disharmony. Both organizations used the same name and logo. I actually made the mistake of trying to mend the rift between the two organizations by agreeing to be on the USA National Coaching Staff for both. I suspect that I only managed to focus their arguments on me rather than doing any good.

Although in 2005, FILA reached an agreement with one of the two organizations to reassume control over the sport, the other organization claims that the two groups were reunified in 2006. At present FILA sanctions international competition in the style, as does FIAS. Both organizations conduct separate world championships and other international events, and it is likely that more political changes may occur.

On July 14, 1995, at the sixth tournament of a new so-called "no-holds-barred" sport, the Ultimate Fighting Championships (VI), a two-time Russian sambo champion astounded the world: Oleg Taktarov. "Sambo is not just a style," observed Taktarov, "but rather a combination of all the best techniques in any self-defense, martial art, and fighting style." Taktarov was not only a Russian sambo champion, but also the four-time, full-contact Euro-Asian jiujitsu champion. He demonstrated and, more important, stated that sambo was an evolving strategy. I observed his fighting style adapt with each new opponent he faced and thus became reinvigorated in my investigation and practice.

What is important is how the above time line merges next, and how the different lineages converged in my own training.

In 1996, I received an invitation from Alexander Ivanovich Retuinskih, a Red Army commander, who was a student and eventually partner of Alexsei Kadochnikov from 1976 to 1982. Retuinskih was a former USSR sambo and judo champion, Distinguished Master of Sport in sambo and judo, Distinguished Coach of Russia, and the founder of "Systema" ROSS (see below).

Alexei Kadochnikov followed Spiridonov's SAMOZ closely, since Kadochnikov was also a professor of engineering. When Retuinskih began to improve on his teaching, Kadochnikov partnered with him in co-research and development. It was at this point that relations between Kadochnikov and Retuinskih became pressured. Kadochnikov believed that competitive resistance did not help improve fighters for combat. It is important to understand Retuinskih's history in order to appreciate the different path his training took from that of Kadochnikov.

When Alexander Retuinskih was 7 years old, he began learning specialized gymnastics/acrobatics, which later formed his interest in biomechanics and psychology. At the age of 12, he began studying boxing; at 14, sambo and combat sambo; and at 19, judo and hand-to-hand fighting. He became a Master of Sport in sambo and judo and a champion of different competitions in Russia and the USSR. In the 1980s, he began researching Russian martial arts. Between 1982 and 1989, he was an instructor of hand-to-hand combat for the police of Krasnodar and Krasnodarskay oblast. It was in 1991, that Kadochnikov and Retuinskih finally split and went different ways.

Beginning in 1991, Retuinskih was the organizer and leader of the International and All-Russian Training—Practical Seminars on RMA. Beginning in 1993 he became chairman of the Russian Combat Sambo Committee of the Russian Sambo Federation and vice chairman of the International Combat Sambo Commission of FIAS (International Sambo Federation) and the general director of the RETAL (Russian Combat Skill Consultant Scientific and Practical Training Center).

In 1995, Alexander Retuinskih patented *Rossijskaya Otechestvennaya Systema Samozashchity,* or ROSS: Russian Native System of Self-Defense. He did this to create a sense of Russian identification and pride, and to create an understanding of Russian martial art as an entire system. But he also did this to differentiate his system from others so that people would understand Retuinskih had devised a unique system of combative education based on his unique study and experience, and that of his research and development team. The ROSS educational system was patented as "Know-How" (registered with the State enterprise "Informpatent" Committee of the Russian Federation by patent and trademark on April 4, 1995).

Beginning in 1997, Retuinskih became the chief of the Department of Hand to Hand Combat for Cossack Military. He was ranked as a general of the Cossack military. With his interaction with the Cossack population came a large influx of interaction with the Cossack folk styles of martial art, such as *Sploch.*

In 1998, at St. Petersburg State Academy of Physical Culture, the Department of Bayonet Fencing and Russian Martial Art ROSS was opened. Retuinskih then wrote a dissertation at the Department of Hand-to-hand Combat of St. Petersburg Military College of Physical Culture, the subject of which was "Methodic ROSS used in teaching." In February of 2000 Retuinskih was awarded the highest award in sports, the Distinguished Coach of Russia.

In 1998, I began working with Boris Shapovalov, Distinguished Master of Sport in Sambo, president of the Ukrainian Federation of Russian-Style Martial Art (Kadochnikov System) and chairman of the Police Sambo Commission for FIAS. With Shapovalov's guidance, I coached the first in history USA Police Sambo Team, competing in the 1999 World Police Sambo Championships in Lithuania. From Shapovalov, an expert in both Kadochnikov's Systema and Retuinskih's ROSS, I came to understand the actual pedagogical differences between the systems of Retuinskih and Kadochnikov.

I also had the honor of training with the last of the royal line of pre-Soviet Russia, the late Prince Boris Golitsin, who in the Great Patriotic War received a maiming bayonet wound to his right shoulder. He composed a fighting system based on his father's teaching of Golitsin family-style (a pre-Soviet, Russian martial art) to accommodate his "disability." After training with him, I would hardly qualify his injury as a disability since with one mostly paralyzed arm, I saw him bayonet-fight three men and have personally felt the pain of his whack. However, this was an independent discipline, having only recently collaborated with ROSS (in the past 10 years).

Retuinskih studied extensively with the famous Alexander Mikhailovich Krivorotov, the first in history Distinguished Coach of Russia in sambo, direct student of Viktor Oshchepkov. Krivorotov, due to Retuinskih's exhaustive research and development, began studying under Retuinskih. I've had the distinct honor of training with Krivorotov. It's difficult to describe to people what it was like training with the world's best sambo coach. Suffice it to say that I learned the difference between amateur and professional training.

Retuinskih also trained with Vladimir V. Volosov, Distinguished Coach of Russia in sambo, chairman of Sambo Academy in Kstovo (the world's largest sambo academy); Vladimir P. Guliaev, Distinguished Coach of Bashkiria in sambo; Uriu A. Shulik, Master of Sport in sambo, doctor of pedagogical sciences, and a current professor of Krasnodar State Academy of Physical Culture; and G. Potoroka, Master of Sport in sambo and judo (deceased).

With my experience with Retuinskih, I gained the final complete picture on sambo: Kharlampievan, Oshchepkovan, and Spiridonovan styles.

Beginning in 1999, I served as vice president of the American Amateur Sambo Federation, the US governing body for the sport of sambo, under the guidance and company of Dr. Leonid Polyakov, FIAS vice president and AASF president, who received a doctorate of physical education through a dissertation on sambo itself. In 1999, he awarded me the Distinguished Master of Sport in SAMBO, the highest achievement in SAMBO, for my contributions to the sport. As a result of our meetings and travels, he connected me with the international leader of sambo, Mikhail Tikhomirov.

At the 1999 annual FIAS board of directors meeting, Dr. Polyakov, FIAS president and All-Russian Sambo Federation president, Mikhail Tikhomirov, FIAS secretary general, and Lithuanian Sambo Federation president Pranciskus Eigminas voted me as the chairman of the International Combat Sambo Commission for FIAS. I was officially inducted to the position that year in Kaunus, Lithuania, during the World Police Sambo Championships.

In 2000, Igor Yakimov, world sambo and judo champion, and North America's highest-rated sambo coach, appointed me as the USA Director of United Federation of Russian Sambo. Yakimov and I worked together for a short time in the attempt to bring combat sambo tournaments to the West.

In 2006, I began coordinating efforts with the American Sambo Association and its president, Stephen Koepfer. Steve remained refreshingly apolitical despite extreme pressures to the contrary and developed his own variation on sport rules called "free-style sambo." This style includes chokes, strangulations, and positional fighting. The development of Steve's organization is another example of evolution in sambo erupting, regardless of oppressive attempts to confine and traditionalize the sport.

THREE RIVERS INTO ONE

I have an interwoven history with sambo and for whatever divine grace was given the opportunity to train only one step removed from each of the founders of sambo—Oshchepkov, Spiridonov, and Kharlampiev, and the three "flavors" or rivers that they created.

From Oshchepkov, we have inherited a practical measuring stick to determine the efficacy of our theories so that no potentially valuable method goes uninvestigated or unevaluated.

From Spiridonov, we have inherited an emphasis on efficiency over effort, on leveraging our strengths and mitigating our weaknesses until such a time that they become strengths.

From Kharlampiev, we have inherited the flexibility to continue our discipline no matter what the format, in whole or in part, so that we can ensure that our legacy will continue to survive.

Each vein of sambo has kept the heart of this creature alive. Although once separate, I believe they are now integrated, each having pumped the life into the content of this book, speaking to you through these pages.

I believe that I have earned the right to say what I believe was the original intent of sambo and to renovate sambo to meet the needs and desires of modern-day fighters. I realize that doing so will not sit well with traditionalists who believe sambo should stay "as it was." They are wrong.

Sambo was never a specific style. It evolved and adapted to the challenges threatening its existence. It survived all the attempts, both foreign and domestic, to squash the methodology from existence. When you read the core doctrine of sambo, you will see why I believe it is directly descended from each of the forefathers of this discipline.

MY PHILOSOPHY OF SAMBO

I've arranged this book in step-by-step format so that you can start at the bottom with technique and work backward up to tactics. The inherent strategies are embedded so that you don't really have to understand them at the beginning. The underlying beliefs are self-explanatory, but if you do under-

RMAX SAMBO

Philosophy Pyramid

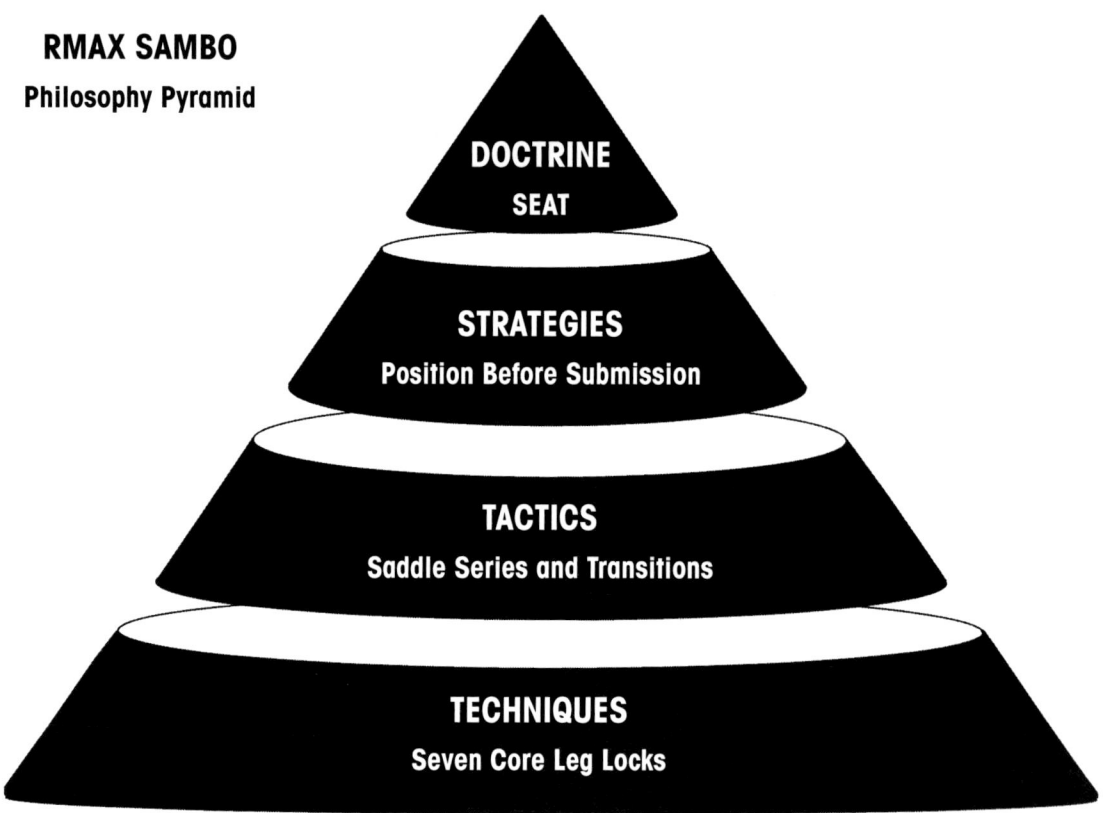

DOCTRINE
SEAT

STRATEGIES
Position Before Submission

TACTICS
Saddle Series and Transitions

TECHNIQUES
Seven Core Leg Locks

SEAT SAMBO DOCTRINE

stand what beliefs created this science, you'll be able to question those beliefs; once you accept them, you can strengthen them.

- *Sustainability.* For a training method to be useful, it must be nondestructive to the practitioner. If you cannot sustain the ability to practice it because it destroys your body, it will not be of any use when you need it.
- *Evolution.* One needs to experience the unexpected and unfamiliar in order to foster continued evolution. Although sound mechanics are universal, training methods must be allowed to evolve as all approaches are relative to the time, culture, and events. Any means necessary to accomplish the task are acceptable. Any potentially valuable method should be weighed and tested on its own merit regardless of origin or association.

- *Aliveness.* To be truly alive, movement, timing, and energy (resistance) are needed. One needs fully alive resistance to become mentally tough and emotionally controlled. Only through actual uncooperative competitive opposition does one truly own knowledge.
- *Transferability.* Good mechanics are universal (context-free), so studying them will allow you adaptability to whatever circumstances you encounter. Regardless of the format, so long as ideas are considered and tested, the adaptation is always organic, never in isolation.

With the "traditionalizing" of sambo, these original intentions have all been neglected, ignored, or redefined in an emasculated manner. I have no taste for it, and stay true to the original intentions listed above.

THE FOUR STRATEGIES OF SAMBO

There are four modes of sambo that are being taught, though they are different from the traditional three flavors of sambo (self-defense, combat, and sport).

SELF-DEFENSE

Self-defense-oriented sambo involves a very large curriculum of techniques resembling stand-up jiujitsu, ground judo, boxing, and kickboxing. Unfortunately, due to the volume of material, there is often not enough time spent facing resistant opponents; this style doesn't claim to be a competitive sphere of martial art. self-defense sambo should remain an adjunct to competitive resistance so that the more fine motor techniques have a platform of timing and rhythm which only alive, dynamic resistance creates within the nervous system. There are many in the West who only train in self-defense sambo, though it was never intended to be trained in, to the exclusion of the other two aspects.

SPORT WRESTLING

Sport sambo is an incredibly athletic game, much like a combination of judo and free-style wrestling, but including leg locks and excluding chokes. However, from its birth to the current day, it remains besieged with politics. From one organization and one event to the next, the rules

are so different that it's difficult to prepare and have a good time. Moreover, the rules have become so restrictive that preparing for sport sambo requires that you become a lesser overall fighter (from a mixed martial arts perspective). Basically, you have to train in dangerous habits, like exposing your neck to strangulation or never developing a good closed guard game.

MIXED MARTIAL ARTS OR COMBAT SAMBO

I know that the traditionalists will be in a tizzy over me saying that one of the flavors of sambo is mixed martial arts (MMA). I say this not because it was a deliberate intention of the founders (although, historically, I could argue that easily, especially since few people truly know the history of sambo), but because it is the mode of actually studying the discipline. When you go to class and work in dynamic drills, you face people of diverse backgrounds, levels, and abilities. With no formalized ranks in combat sambo, everyone fights everyone. What I'm saying here is that the mode in which combat sambo is studied is more important than the content of the actual class: facing other martial artists of mixed backgrounds. This is the superiority of combat sambo as a delivery system for timing and rhythm, the essential virtues of fighting efficacy.

SPETSNAZ COMBAT SAMBO OR SYSTEMA

Since Soviet special purpose units ("Spetsnaz") training held the condition of "absolute secrecy," the nebulous designation of "systema" (the system) was assigned to special

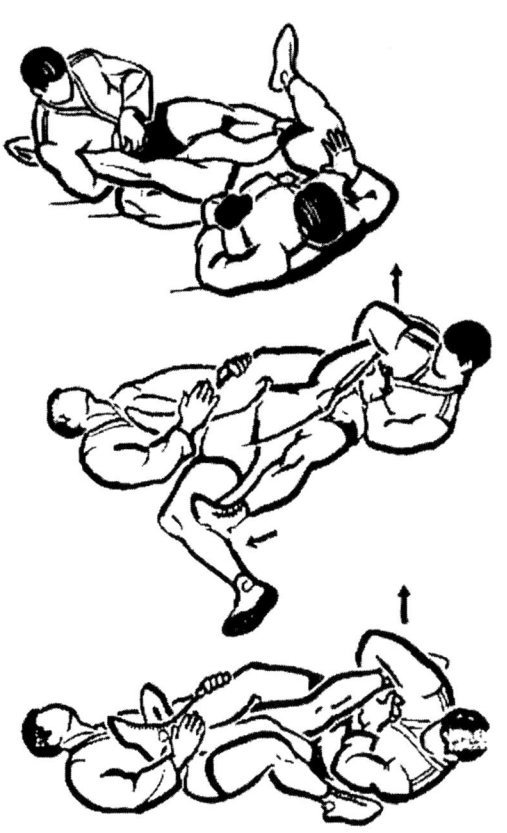

forces combatives training. A prominent reference call-sign was combat sambo Spetsnaz. During the fall of the Soviet Union, many trainers were left in the field to fend for themselves. As a result, we saw the emergence of a diverse amount of styles appear such as *Vyzhivaniya* (survival), *Rukopashni Boi* (hand-to-hand combat), *Kulachni Boi* (hand-to-hand fighting) as Alexander Retuinskih's Systema, Alexey Kadochnikov's Systema, and Mikhail Ryabko's Systema. Although I had extensive training in Spetsnaz combat sambo, it is a military specific discipline that includes a wide array of tools and tradecraft beyond the scope of nonmilitary personnel.

I find sambo for MMA, or combat sambo, to be the most athletically stimulating, intellectually challenging, and personally/professionally fulfilling of the categories. When I'm discussing tactics and techniques, I am only speaking of fighting other martial artists, not sport-wrestling or self-defense.

Originally, these three flavors were meant to be synergistic, but, frankly, most nonprofessionals do not have the time, energy, or inclination to practice all three. Most people aren't familiar enough with sport-wrestling sambo to be interested, and most will not invest the long years of practice to refine the self-defense aspects of sambo. This book, however, deals specifically with combat sambo and its stage in the mixed martial arts world.

CHAPTER 5

SAMBO'S TACTICAL CONTRIBUTION: LEG-TO-LEG ATTACKS

There are basically four dimensions to submission grappling:

- Arms-to-arms attacks—the realm of Greco-Roman wrestling
- Arms-to-legs attacks—the realm of folk-style, free-style, and even catch wrestling
- Legs-to-arms attacks—the realm of jiujitsu and judo
- Legs-to-legs attacks—the realm of sambo

For a solid MMA game, at least in submission grappling, you need (at minimum) the following:

- a good clinch
- a good shot/sprawl
- a good guard
- a good leg ride

When I say arms, I am referring to the solar plexus; and when I say legs, I mean the lunar plexus. It's not just arms and legs (and not really arms and legs at all).

I grade my athletes so they know where they should be working, on a scale of 1 to 10 on each of their games. For example, one athlete may have a technique game of 6 in Greco, 6 in free-style, 3 in jiujitsu, and 8 in sambo. It's his jiujitsu that makes him vulnerable in this example, so that's what he needs to shore up in his practice. I outsource my staff and bring in the best coaches from any sport to get the job done for my fighters.

Sambo primarily contributes leg-to-leg attacks in MMA. Even though sambo has mount, side mount, cross-side, north-south, guard, half-guard, turtle, and back mount, what is currently almost absent in the MMA world—a temporary "hole" in the sport as a community—is in one family of positions in particular: the leg rides.

Sambo's sport-wrestling restrictions have perverted the training method into a fast-wrestling approach rather than a slow, methodical one. In general, sambo fighters are like the rabbit and not the turtle. That works fine against other sambo sport-wrestlers, against most traditional martial artists, and against 20 percent of the MMA community. I personally don't like those odds.

I realize that some sport sambo experts have suggested that if MMA athletes would know "proper" leg locks, they would apply them fast enough to finish. The fast leg lock is the urban myth of mixed martial arts competition. Though there have been quite a few world sambo champions in MMA, even they have no greater than a 20 percent average of finishing with fast-wrestling leg locks.

The purpose of this book is to show that it's not the speed of application that's the problem. It's starting the lock from position. When I refer to a family of positions that I lump under the category of leg rides, I am not saying most sambo athletes train this way. I'm only saying that I train my athletes this way.

I no longer speak for sambo as an international organization. I speak now only for my sambo; our combat sambo concentration in the modern world of mixed martial arts competition.

With that disclaimer out of the way, I'll explain how you can include this new family of positions into your submission fighting repertoire to take advantage of a temporary, rapidly disappearing hole in the MMA game; to open yourself up to a vast array of leg locks; and to increase your percentage of success in effectively applying them against the difficult 80 percent of the athletes you'll be facing, in class and competition.

CHAPTER 6

SAMBO SINCE 1980

When I speak of sambo's evolution in the past two decades since the popularization of mixed martial art "competitions," I am only speaking about my personal experience and the evolution of my approach. I am not suggesting that any other practitioners—especially classic traditionalists—have to, or desire to, evolve their approaches.

Some people practice the discipline exactly as it was when it was formalized in 1938. To me that's insane. Think how much fighting tactics have evolved in the past 20 years alone! Despite commercial attempts at traditionalizing sambo, it has for the most part remained renegade and true to the spirit, not the dogma, of the discipline. I reach out to you maverick practitioners to stay plugged in to each other so that we can continue to flourish and maintain our evolution, in spite of marketplace seductions forcing us into the codified rubber stamp of strip-mall dojos.

My combat sambo approach was forced to evolve because fast-wrestling (the belief in attempting submission before position) has some inherent holes in it due to the advent of the slower, much more methodical Brazilian Jiujitsu approach of position before submission.

In sport-wrestling (sambo), with only one six-minute match, and the ability to win on takedowns and throw point superiority with only 60 seconds of action permitted on the ground, submission attempts can come out of nowhere and be applied very quickly. That's fine when no striking is involved, and no choking is permitted. But once you open up the game to striking and choking, fast-wrestling can lead to trouble. Jiujitsu taught me that in 1992, when I first got to work with Rigan Machado at National Sambo Championships (where he won his entire division). He gave up the four-point throw, pulled an open guard, gave up the four-point hold down, and used the 60 seconds on the ground to land arm-bar after arm-bar, despite not being able to close guard or choke (which were against sambo sport-wrestling rules).

In jiujitsu, we're taught to move inch by inch, closing up the "slop" (all of the wasted space); to wear our opponent like our own rash-guard. Although jiujitsu teaches us an amazing array of technical possibilities, it's this attention to mechanical detail that forced my game to evolve as a fighter and as a coach. Why? Because eight times out of ten, the athlete trained to be slow and methodical will beat the athlete trained to be fast and fickle. Two times out of ten, everyone gets a "boxer's chance" at landing an unorthodox submission. But, personally, I don't like those odds.

The most positive attribute of combat sambo has been its focus on facing fighters of different training backgrounds. Even in the early years of combat sambo tournaments in Russia, the reinvigoration of original mixed-style fighting continued combat sambo's distinction as a fighting craft rather than merely a wrestling sport. Seeing those early matches of "Russian combat sambo wrestling versus the World" as a collision of two strategies was very illuminating and recharted my study for the next decade.

I started studying mixed-fight competitions in the early 1990s. Understanding combat sambo's roots, despite its disparate modes and divergent "rivers," I had no qualms about reinvigorating my combat sambo with jiujitsu, Greco-Roman, free-style, folk-style, and even the nearly-antiquated catch wrestling. I consider myself a sambo practitioner at my core, because I internalize the doctrine, and because it's now impossible to extract its strategies and tactics from the manner in which I, and my athletes, fight.

FAST VERSUS POSITIONAL SUBMISSION FIGHTING

Sport sambo wrestling is "fast" wrestling: only 60 seconds allowed on the ground, and only if there is visible action toward a sub (submission). With no closed guard and no hold-down points after the initial 20 seconds once per match, wrestlers are encouraged to jump for subs rather than set them up positionally. As a result, even in the combat (fighting) sport, positional fighting was discouraged.

Fast wrestling (such as in sanshou, catch-as-catch-can, *kurash*, and kodokan judo) works fine against other fast wrestlers. However, a positional grappler nullifies that to a major extent because, while in a position, there is heavy compression of top fighter to bottom. It's highly rare for a bottom fighter to be able to land a "fast" sub. Even if a fighter has top control, if he leaps to a sub against a bottom player who practices positional fighting, he'll most likely not get the sub and probably be reversed if not in a sub immediately himself. Fast-wrestling subs only land about 20 percent of the time.

THE SCRAMBLE

Positional dominance and maintenance take longer to learn than the free-style/folk-style wrestling "scramble" because positional grappling isn't based on athleticism. The scramble works well in the early years, but eventually methodical grappling will eliminate any lifting edge that the scramble needs for escape. As a result, grappling must evolve into a more sophisticated game, because athleticism wanes with age, whereas technique only continues to mature.

The scramble can expose you to surprise submissions because by definition you lose control of not only your opponent, but also yourself. Scrambling for a leg submission most often exposes you to cross-side bottom if not exposing your back completely. It's rarely advisable for the leg game, and I'd never endorse it for a primary strategy. However, from a practical standpoint, I still keep my scramble in my competitive toolbox as an option, if at any point I'm outclassed technically.

WHY LEG LOCKS ARE LESS COMMON THAN ARM LOCKS

Unfortunately, most people have learned leg attacks from sport sambo fast wrestling. They must sacrifice good position in order to leap for an ankle, foot, or knee. Good fighters are not seduced by the attractiveness of a low-percentage submission hold. Instead, they'll slowly and methodically maintain position, surfing from one to the next, until the opponent overcommits in his attempt to escape or counter. Then, and only then, they'll take the submission.

Only against inferior opponents do "exotic" submissions have any value. Even then, why not concentrate on developing the basics even more? It's very embarrassing to lose to an inferior opponent just because you were trying to be "fancy."

Leg attacks have been historically excluded from jiujitsu for cultural reasons. It's still frowned upon, or at least not looked highly upon in Brazil. It does not help that historically, sport jiujitsu and submission grappling competitions based on jiujitsu award such significant points (4) to passing the guard. This has historically discouraged the refinement of a lower-half game, by the very nature of the rules.

In Russia, contrarily, sambo suffered because to "go to one's knees" is a cultural stigma. Avoiding going to one's knees is built into the rule set of sambo, which is why in Russia, it's been historically taught as a throwing art rather than a ground-fighting art. In sambo, going to one's knees—or, worse, to one's back—results in loss of points or loss of match, to reflect the strong cultural stigma against falling to one's knees.

In all the sambo gyms I trained in throughout the former Soviet Union, we never began grappling on our knees. As a result, the technical ground wizardry of Brazilian Jiujitsu (BJJ) was more sophisticated in the upper-half game than in native Russian sambo.

Fortunately, sambo can throw or take down to positional dominance. However, as we saw in the early years of popular MMA competitions, fighters began to adapt strategies to combat that approach (such as the "guard flop") and, as a result, nullified a great deal of leg attacks.

Combat sambo had to respond to the advent of Brazilian Jiujitsu by fighting positionally as well. For instance, the average BJJ fighter will do better at escaping conventional sambo leg attacks than the average sambo fighter. Although I'm sure such a comment may curdle the milk of traditional sambo instructors, it's the stark, painful truth.

In jiujitsu, the elaborate technical education of passing the guard translates with only a few months of practice into passing sambo leg attacks that are secured only by the knee pinch. However, with sambo, there are no points

awarded for passing the guard and leg attacks are legal. As a result, combat sambo has developed a sophisticated array of leg counters and counter-counter attacks. But positional transitions escaping leg attack positions are not remotely as common. The conventional sambo fast-lock, knee-pinch isolation is low-percentage in jiujitsu and, as a result, mixed martial arts competition (where BJJ has established itself as a dominant force).

A large portion of sambo leg attacks, however, focused on isolating the hips positionally. They concentrated on first controlling the lower half of the body, then working outward from hip to knee to ankle. This approach had a very high percentage success rate in submission fighting. These tactics worked especially well against fighters who were not familiar with an opponent who did not attempt to pass their guard, but rather attacked the guard as an opportunity.

Like good jiujitsu anchors and controls the solar plexus, to attack the arms and neck, good sambo must secure and anchor the lunar plexus (hips/pelvis/lower back/core) to attack the hips, knees, ankles, and feet—in that order. This is not to presume that sambo does not attack the upper half or that jiujitsu doesn't attack the lower half, but rather that they concentrate study on their respective domains and work toward the other direction.

FACING OPPONENTS FOSTERS EVOLUTION

Free-wrestling (nonpositional) leg attacks in MMA result from a traditional bias against them in BJJ. It's the rules of both sports—sport sambo and sport jiujitsu—that injure the effectiveness of both disciplines.

If leg attacks hadn't been looked down upon in traditional jiujitsu, I would expect that BJJ would have a more sophisticated leg attack game than sambo because BJJ focuses on the superior concept of positional dominance and maintenance, whereas sambo historically has focused on free or "fast" submission wrestling (submission without position.) Due to the traditional bias against leg attacks, when BJJ did start to incorporate them more aggressively, it was/is done without creating new positional requirements.

The positional fighting for leg attacks must be built outward from the ground floor of the other essential positions: guard, half-guard, cross-side, north/south, head/arm, mount, side mount and knee-on-belly.

I call these full saddle, side saddle, rear saddle, and reverse saddle. In traditional sambo wrestling, they're known as leg lace, leg lariat, and leg knot, but these are more of a wrestling "leg ride" due to the speed of sambo fast-wrestling.

In the mixed martial arts world, no current Russian sambo approach will be complete without intensively researching and studying Brazilian Jiujitsu for its superior positional dominance and maintenance. I hope that this book rectifies that problem.

Not just from a grappling standpoint, but also from a striking standpoint, much of classic sambo striking derives its force purely from circular/angular "looping" torque rather than from the ground rooting typified in "Western" boxing; this is analogous to fast-wrestling versus positional grappling. Combat sambo's striking has improved as a result of having to evolve to face positional fighters.

CHAPTER 7

UPPER AND LOWER HALVES RESTORED

I love seeing successful combat sambo fighters showing that the discipline can evolve, rid itself of institutionalized limitations, and continue to address the reality of fight sport.

Combat sambo for me has evolved not merely in content, but in composition: how you study it is just as, if not more, important than what is studied. The slow, methodical game of "removing slop" is the way I approach preparing my fighters. In other words, even though my primary base is sambo, I still adhere to the position-before-submission approach.

For instance, my combat sambo evolved because of facing other martial artists. In sport sambo, the knee pinch leg isolation works because other sambo athletes won't try to pass the weak isolation, but mirror it and attempt their own lock. However, a knee pinch on a BJJ athlete will be quickly passed. This brought me into the jiujitsu upper-half game and virtually eliminated my sambo lower-half game.

I had to develop two directions as a result:

- Develop my upper-half game so that I could navigate my way back to my lower-half game.
- Develop positional strength in my lower-half game to prevent the other fighters from passing to upper-half game.

The first task is obvious. I got to work. There's a lifetime of study in just one art, with much, much more for all four dimensions. However, I learned enough to get my head inside the strategy to see where the connection was to the lower-half game, where I was at home.

My study continues to expand so that I can find my way technically back to the lower-half from farther and farther away.

I'm finding that this is also helping as my athletes get more sophisticated in their lower-half strategy. I have to move to upper-half fighting as they continue to refine their lower-half game. That forces me to set up any lower-half attacks farther away in moves by credible upper-half game attacks. It's a win-win situation because we're all growing, and the game continues to be so damn fun.

The second half was not so immediately obvious. In combat sambo, there are more secure leg isolations, called the leg lariat and leg lace. But these are not preferred by most athletes due to the fast-wrestling approach. However, in positional fighting, I found these to be stronger and to have huge potential.

I had to adapt the leg lariat and leg lace into the saddle and side saddle, respectively, by adjusting the leg triangle to thwart the sweeps and passes jiujitsu athletes were applying. This required finding security against the mat with the under-hooked leg, and safety underneath his body with the over-hooked leg.

In essence, you need to be able to fight positional passes with your under-hooked leg's knee and hip, while simultaneously defending your over-hooked leg's foot by burying it in the nooks and crannies of his lower half. That's how the family of positions associated with the saddle developed.

I can't take credit for the mechanics, though we've created a growing list of very cool leg attacks, transitions, sweeps, and entries. However, I can accept credit for the exciting new perspective of converting the leg lace and leg lariat into a positional fighting approach.

A FINAL WORD ABOUT NAMES

The names you encounter in this book are the nicknames adopted by my athletes; they could be Japanese proper names, American historical names, Russian translations, or even colloquial monikers for things we made up. If you ask me purely by name, I may not even remember what you're talking about because they just blend together in my head. I'm only able to break these down in class so that we have technical examples.

CHAPTER 8

SADDLE POSITION

In sambo, the arrangement of the legs lacing across the attacked leg is traditionally called the leg lariat.

The saddle is based on this position, but it is a position that I was forced to develop as a result of facing martial artists of mixed backgrounds, in particular against those trained with good jiujitsu: the methodical, positional approach. I did not create the concept of isolating the leg, which comes from classic sambo wrestling. However, to implement it into mixed martial arts, the mechanics involved applying it to MMA, and its seamless integration within positional submission fighting, is something that I feel honored to have contributed.

Although a *good* lower-half game would be sufficient against nonfighters and most novice fighters, you need to develop a refined upper-half game if you want to develop a *great* lower-half game. Attacking farther and farther away from the lower half, adapting and recovering from fast scrambles that leave you at the upper half, and understanding the intricate wizardry of the guard and how it will be used in an effort to thwart your saddle, demand that you have a well-rounded upper and lower game.

That being said, I'm obviously better with my lower-half game than my upper, at the writing of this book. I continue to work to resolve that disparity in both skill and coaching. However, for most submission fighting athletes, the lower-half game is little to none.

My coaching strategy for submission grappling holds the saddle as one of its flagship tactics and showcases it in most of our leg locks as the position before submission in leg attacks. So, let's begin by describing the primary mechanics before we discuss how to transition into it.

There are four standard variations to the saddle position: the full saddle, side saddle, rear saddle, and reverse saddle. We will primarily address the full saddle in this book.

CHAPTER 9

PRIMARY MECHANICS

All variations of the saddle involve four movement tactics:

- Fire pole

- Leg triangle

- Tourniquet

- Lock

FIRE POLE

The failure of most leg lock attempts comes from viewing the leg as an arm. Many novice athletes make the mistake of trying to apply an arm lock without securing the solar plexus and then the shoulder of the arm to be attacked. This mistake is even more frequent when attacking the legs. I have observed that this is due to the free-wrestling approach to leg locks.

To transform your leg locks into a positional fighting approach, you must secure the hips and pelvis, which we'll call the lunar plexus.

Bottom side control of the lunar plexus.

Securing the lunar plexus should not require a great deal of effort, since good Jiujitsu always secures the near and far hip in mount, cross-side, and knee-on-diaphragm. Understanding how to open the opponent's legs to attack while securing the lunar plexus requires a special movement that I call the fire pole.

The fire pole involves hugging the opponent's thigh to your chest and scooting your sits bones as high up his leg toward his hips as possible. The action of sliding the opponent's thigh up your chest by lifting the opponent's knee toward your head, while scooting your hips toward his own, looks much like a fireman sliding down the fire pole from the second floor of the fire station.

Hug and scoot.

The hug-and-scoot movement (knee pinch, hike up fire pole) should always precede the lock in order to isolate your opponent's hip, but it can also be used to tighten the hold, throw from standing or sweep from the ground, transition to a different lock, or block the opponent's attempt to break your position.

Once you slide as high as possible up the "fire pole," it's time to lock on the leg triangle.

LEG TRIANGLE

Jiujitsu and MMA fighters will recognize this technique immediately from attacks to the head and arms. The leg triangle to attack the leg must be modified from arm and head attack mechanics, because when attacking the legs the leg triangle must:

- secure the hip fold of the attacked leg with your under-laced shin;
- anchor the knee of the under-laced leg to the ground in your opponent's ribs (in full saddle) or under his crotch (in side saddle);
- protect the foot of the over-laced leg under the opponent's sits bones (in full saddle) or floating ribs (in side saddle).

Although the leg triangle, by sight and by name, appears to be merely the position of your legs on your opponent's attacked leg, it's much more about how to fight with your knees to block and with your hips to control your opponent's movement.

You need to learn how to fight behind the knee on the mat, and how to use your hips to stay in the saddle, once your opponent starts to apply resistance. If you start with light resistance, concentrate on holding position through knee blocks and hip heists to control him.

Don't look for the submissions. Those come last, once you know how to control him, or how to "ride in the saddle." Just like in the jiujitsu top-half game, when you're comfortable "surfing" in position, then you'll see that no matter where your opponent moves, he must expose one or more of the core leg-lock submissions.

TOURNIQUET

What you cannot see from the photo below is the tourniquet effect that the saddle applies to the opponent's thigh. It should feel like you're strangling his thigh between your legs. The tourniquet's power begins with the leg triangle. As you lace on the figure-4, you create what I call a "slipknot" to tighten your instep as

Leg triangle from full saddle; under-lace in hip fold.

Knee in, ribs on mat.

Over-lace between sits bones.

deeply as possible into the back of your knee pit. You do this by swinging your over-lacing leg in a small crescent and then backward to finalize the triangle.

Your over-laced leg's heel is pulling back toward your own butt. Your knees are squeezing together. You're pulling his knee as high up toward your head as possible, while simultaneously using that leverage to pull your butt down his thigh bone, like sliding down a fireman's pole.

The squeeze.

This squeeze is hard to describe, and unless you've actually experienced it, it's hard to imagine. The tourniquet is the "riding control" of the saddle. It's how you stay in the saddle as the opponent moves. Now, positionally, this is much like a leg triangle attack to the solar plexus from the guard. It can be ridden from bottom to top to side control.

CYCLING THROUGH ADJUSTMENTS

When fighting, you will find that you will cycle through these four tactics very fast, without thought, and in the order necessary to tighten the hold slowly and methodically, until you land the final lock.

Sometimes you slip too low on the leg and must apply the "scoot up the fire pole" technique to get deeper. Sometimes your opponent unlaces your leg triangle, so you must release the tourniquet to reposition, roll, sweep, and relace. Often the lock isn't in place. so instead of fighting for it, you abandon it, sink higher up the fire pole, tighten or adjust your leg triangle, apply the tourniquet more tightly, and wait for the submission to appear.

LEG PUMMELING

Although you can end the fight with a submission by doing so, learning how to pummel your arms and legs together to form triangles on your opponent's leg is crucial to understanding the saddle game.

Pummeling is a game most associated with stand-up grappling in the clinch. However, I use the term for whenever you weave your limbs in, out, and around your opponent's limbs in order to secure positional control. Therefore, I also include pummeling as a concept for fighting to establish a lock-down on the opponent's bottom half.

There are as many variations of leg-pummeling configurations as there are styles of "guard" in jiujitsu.

The Crank
I had to come up with the crank because when you move to lace in your leg triangle on jiujitsu fighters, they're used to defending it and trying to pass it like a guard.

You have your lace over his hip fold, but you have not yet gotten your other leg lacing over it to secure the triangle. If you move your over-lacing leg long and high over the top of your leg triangle, he can defend well.

However, if you take your free arm (the one not securing his attacked leg under the armpit) and grab the foot of your shin in his hip fold, you not only can crank it down under your knee to lock in the leg triangle without ever extending your leg, but you can also use it as a temporary triangle to secure his attacked leg, until the second leg arrives to finalize the leg triangle.

High leg over (do not do!).

Reach under crank.

Even if you cannot lock in the leg triangle, you are still in a "weak" triangle, which may be sufficient to either finish, or transition to a deeper position or the next hold.

Bandolier

The bandolier is most often a temporary position where you are substituting your free arm until you can get your top leg laced on. It

happens often when you're too high up the calf with your attacking arm, and/or too low down your opponent's thigh with your hips.

Basic position.

Grab hold of your over-laced foot with your free hand. Keeping your attacking arm under your opponent's leg, lace your hand over the forearm of the arm grabbing your foot. In the bandolier, you can often fire-pole up higher back into the saddle, and then transition back into the crank so that you can complete the leg triangle without your arms.

Fire-pole and crank.

Often the bandolier is a good temporary solution to an opponent who is attempting to roll out before you have the full saddle on. Just hold on and wait for the opportunity to crank or complete the lace as he frees your position to do so.

Rustler

The side saddle makes your outside, over-hooking leg vulnerable because it remains within reach of your opponent's arms. If he catches your leg, he can unlace your leg triangle or even occasionally land a low-percentage, "fast" lock on your foot or ankle.

To address this, I developed a technique for securing the free leg deeply under your own leg triangle. If you're inflexible or injured, it may not even be possible. But my Prasara yoga and Intu-Flow mobility practice (prehabilitative fitness approach to lubricationg the joints and connective tissue) have allowed my joints to become healthy enough to handle more dramatic techniques like the rustler.

While in the side saddle, lock down your leg triangle as deeply as possible toward your opponent's hip.

Lying on your side with your knee down between his legs, take your outside, top-side arm

Reach under.

and grab your free leg ankle. Pull it back as far as possible.

With your other arm, reach between your legs and underneath your opponent's trapped leg and grab your ankle with your other hand.

Pull to lotus.

Pull it underneath toward his sits bones as much as possible, into a half lotus.

From this position, you're relatively safe from him passing your leg triangle. Even if you cannot hold it there for long and attack his trapped leg, it can buy you sufficient time to finish the lock on his leg.

Double Triangle

You get the double triangle when you're applying the knee pinch, in preparation for the transition for the saddle, and your opponent crosses his legs (or if he feeds you his free leg).

Reach up and slide his foot down toward his hip fold. Then lace over his crossed leg.

You can drive back and finish him from here. However, if you fire-pole down toward his thigh, you will sink in the hip submission much tighter on your opponent, to "cock the hammer" on the finishing hold.

Apply the leg triangle again with your other leg over your ankle from the bottom, for the side saddle.

Knee pinch with leg feed.

Lace over his crossed leg and cock the hammer.

Lock in the double triangle.

Gordian Knot

The Gordian knot happens when you shoot your shin over into your opponent's hip fold for full saddle, and he rotates his knee inward in order to defend.

Use your far arm to help under-hook his far knee with your over-lacing foot.

Apply your far knee over his over-lacing leg and cross your ankle underneath.

This is a finishing move, because as you sit up on your post and extend your legs, you submit his knee and hip simultaneously.

Inward knee rotation.

Scoop the far knee and under-hook with your foot.

Lace over.

CHAPTER 10

BASIC SADDLE VARIATIONS

Besides the full saddle, there are three additional basic variations of the saddle position: side saddle, rear saddle, and reverse saddle.

SIDE SADDLE

The leg position in the side saddle is traditionally called the leg lace, though I was forced to create the mechanics of locking this down as a position to increase the percentage of success in leg locks when facing positional grapplers.

The fire pole still applies, but because your sits bones are on the outside of your opponent's thigh rather than on the inside like the primary saddle, you will be forced to apply the tourniquet more tightly.

The side saddle mechanics are similar in that a leg triangle is placed around the thigh of the leg you intend to attack. However, your inside leg laces over the opponent's thigh to the outside of his hip, and then that ankle under your outside leg's knee.

Optimally, you want to roll on your side so that your opponent's leg you're attacking remains trapped underneath your torso, while simultaneously bringing the foot of your outside leg behind his bottom to defend your own leg. Your inside knee should be between his thighs with your shin in his hip fold so that you can effectively prevent his escape by extending your hips and applying force through your shin into his hips.

Side saddle with rustled leg.

Nonpositional leg lock counterattempt.

This move creates a somewhat vulnerable position for your outside leg. It is mostly susceptible to nonpositional foot locks, or if your opponent can bump your foot across his centerline to his far shoulder, you could be exposed to ankle, Achilles, or heel hooks. That is true, if he has the time.

If he tries to scoop your outside leg to his near shoulder, your knee leaks leverage. As he applies a lock to your foot, your knee can release the pressure upward. All the while, you're attacking his saddled leg. This is a perfect example of the difference between free-wrestling and positional fighting leg lock games.

Leg triangle stall.

If you remain on your back, and your opponent defends well with wrist control, he may be able to bump his own saddled leg foot across and lace it under his free leg. This is a stalling position.

The mechanics of the crank, bandolier, and rustler still apply in the side saddle.

REAR SADDLE

A rear saddle, also known as the twister or banana split, is traditionally called the leg ride. It refers to lacing your leg triangle in from the back position (your back to his belly). Commonly entered from the turtle in jiujitsu or *par terre* base in wrestling, it is mostly used as a sweep, rather than a position." To be used as a position requires that the mechanics be modified from its free-wrestling origin.

Back mounting with rear saddle.

Rear Saddle Basic Entry
Make your opponent bear weight on his back. Fake the ankle pick to load the upper half. If he rolls under to pull guard, maintain your grasp on his ankle and you'll land him knee-on-diaphragm, ready to enter the saddle.

If your opponent posts outward to block the turnover, he'll expose his legs to entering the rear saddle. Lift the inserted leg shin high into the hip

1. Fake ankle pick.

2. If he posts, lock in the triangle. Pick the ankle.

3a and b. Hook the thigh.

fold to secure the saddle before rolling him over. Lock in the leg triangle as you pick his far ankle. When you pick his ankle, insert your opposite arm to the center of the inside of his thigh.

Many different submissions can be enabled from this position, but concentrating on the seven core finishes will give you the ability to be creative.

4. If he rolls to guard, control ankle to knee-on-diaphragm with leg control.

5. Banana split roll.

6. Knee slice variation.

Reverse saddle.

REVERSE SADDLE

A reverse saddle refers to a situation where your body position is upside down; your back is toward your opponent's belly, and your crotch is over the top of his quadriceps and your leg triangle under his hamstring.

The reverse saddle appears often, but most notably when you are attacking your opponent from turtle bottom.

This is a frequent defense against belly-to-back throws, which is outside the scope of this book since I'm concentrating on introducing the positional ground-fighting aspect of my

1. Your turtle position is attacked.

2. Reach between, scoop his leg, and roll.

3. Lock in reverse saddle for knee bar.

sambo; I do offer some standing grappling saddle attacks.

Your leg triangle tends to be much safer here because of the difficulty your opponent has in trying to reach behind his back to break your leg lace. It's not foolproof, though. You need to have a deep fire pole and strong tourniquet so that he can't attack your back. If you execute the reverse saddle correctly, he won't be able to attack your back effectively.

You will find that there is a very tight transition between full, side, and reverse saddle. If you change the degree that you spin on his attacked thigh, or if he rolls within your leg

triangle with a loose tourniquet, you can transition between positions very quickly and efficiently. But doing so takes long practice. Focus on the basics in this book. Let the "fancy" attacks happen as an outgrowth of your mastery of the saddle basics.

Traditional sambo uses two additional positions, which are structurally weak compared with the saddle family: the knee pinch and double-knee pinch. They can, though, be used as transitional positions to move to the saddles. They can also be used as temporary rescue positions to prevent escapes when the opponent clears your leg triangle.

1. Execute a standing reap between his legs.

2. Roll and grab your own ankle.

3. Reverse saddle and lace in figure-four knee slice.

The knee pinch and double-knee pinch truly come into your game once you've mastered precision with your leg attacks through positional dominance and maintenance. When you've sufficiently practiced the locks with the significant structure of the saddles, you'll find that your increased precision will require less and less structure, thereby making the knee pinches feasible. I highly encourage you to not fight from the knee pinches until you practice the saddles for a year or two. Use them only as transitions, rescues, or escape counters until you become laser-precise with your leg locks.

KNEE PINCH

The pinch is the classic isolation of the opponent's leg, but it's extremely weak compared to the saddle family, because only tension holds your opponent's leg in place. With a sharp knee-to-chest pull, and backward roll, he can free himself. With some intelligent scramble, most strong athletes can free their leg from the pinch.

attacked leg until the full saddle or side saddle can be laced in.

To increase your percentage of success, once you apply the pinch, do the following:

1. Before you roll to your side holding his leg, butterfly lift his far knee to create space.
2. While rolling to your side, lace your leg over his hip fold.
3. Lace in the leg triangle. Get your knee to the ground, fire-pole up, rustle in your far leg, and apply the tourniquet.
4. Fire-pole and apply the tourniquet.
5. While you attempt the above, if your opponent rolls to his belly, surf with him, and as his roll frees the first leg, lace it over; when it frees the second leg, finalize the leg triangle.
6. The submission is last, in this example with an Achilles lock.

Anywhere along this process you will have a chance to finish him, but you will not be as certain as having established the full position.

Knee pinch, feet tucked.

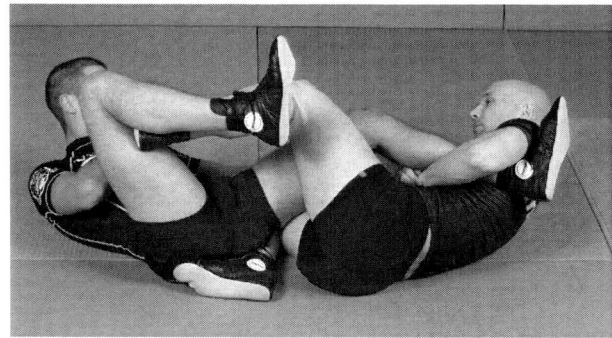

1. Butterfly clear far knee.

2. Lace in hip fold.

To prevent easy sweeps and gain some hip control, tuck both of your feet into the contour of his body. Your inside foot tucks between his sits bones, and your outside foot inwardly rotates and tucks under his buttocks.

The pinch does happen quite often, or at least the opportunities appear often. When they do, the pinch may be sufficient to anchor the

3a and b. Leg triangle and tourniquet

4. Fire pole and squeeze.

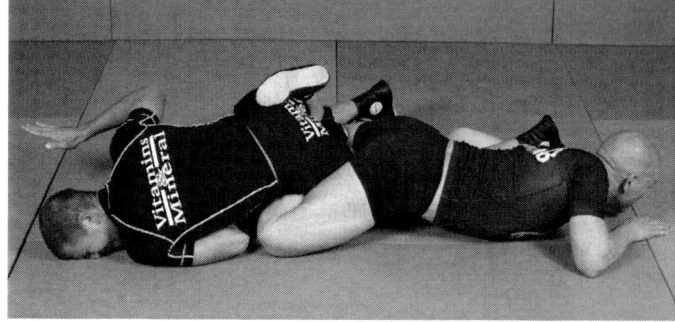

5. Roll to belly.

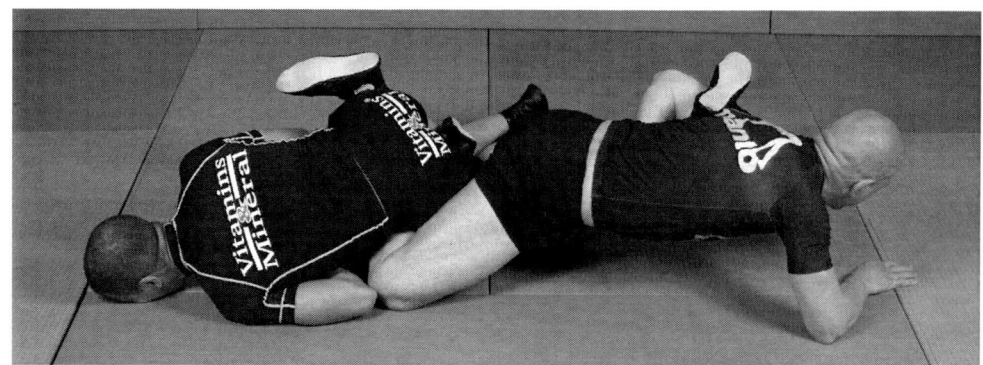

6. Achilles lock.

Passing the Knee Pinch

The average jiujitsu fighter will be more proficient at passing the knee pinch than the average sambo fighter, because the former adapts his guard passing game to the knee pinches (though they're very difficult to adapt against the saddles). Again, this is due to the nature of each respective game: BJJ encourages guard passing by awarding high points for doing so, and doesn't permit leg locks. Sambo permits attacking the legs and doesn't

STRUCTURAL STRENGTH AND CHANCE OF SUCCESS	
TECHNIQUE	CHANCE OF SUCCESS
Free-wrestling lock	20%
Basic knee pinch	50%
First-leg half triangle	60%
Second-leg full triangle	70%
Fire pole; apply tourniquet	85%
Lock down knee; bury foot	95%

1. Roll up as he rolls back, hands on his knees, shin tucked.

2a and b. Shin rock.

3. Knee pass to standing mount.

permit closed guard or chokes, and hence there is no encouragement to pass the guard. The rules for BJJ and sambo have changed, and the advent of open submission fighting, combat sambo, and MMA competitions have changed this so that may no longer be the case for some fighters.

Jiujitsu fighters tend to be spastic when you attack their legs due to their unfamiliarity and, as a result, neglect to adapt their guard passing skills. Combat sambo fighters, contrarily, don't have a problem learning new skills and freely adopt whatever works from any discipline or sport. As a result, they have developed innovative guard games.

I'll show you a few knee pinch passes that you will be able to pull off pretty easily once you practice these two core knee pinch pass mechanics.

Shin Rock

Imagine that someone attempted to hold you in his guard by merely pinching his knees against your ribs. You'd laugh, right? And yet, that's how leg attacks are primarily taught in traditional sport sambo and, as a result, Brazilian Jiujitsu, submission fighting, and MMA. Many jiujitsu fighters are so concerned about leg locks that they will forget all their guard passing skills and get nailed in an easily passable lock.

The shin rock happens as the knee pinch is applied and the opponent begins to roll back to go for the lock. Place your hands on his knees, and tuck your opposite leg in toward your bottom.

Pointing your toes, roll up onto your shin by letting the opponent's roll back pull you up.

You can continue this motion to place your attacked foot flat on the mat, while pulling his knees back to pass up and over to mount. Make sure you clear the down knee between your legs so that he can't sufficiently block the pass.

Knee Block Pummel Against the Wishbone Block

In traditional sport sambo, there's a wishbone block, in which your opponent forces your far leg away by pushing into your knee pit with his foot.

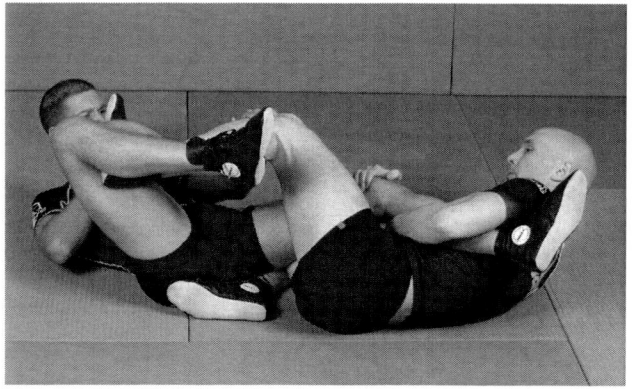

1. Wishbone block.

2. Reach up and grab your own ankle.

3. Lever off your opponent's leg and clear your own free.

4. Trap across his leg and finish him.

You can easily remove his brace. For flexible fighters, just continue your split, grab your own ankle, and lever your leg and up and over his. If you're not flexible, reach under your thigh with your near arm, and lace your hand over his ankle.

With that lever, move your leg quickly out as you pry up on your thigh and crank down on his ankle.

Don't worry about your flexibility because your ballistic range of motion is greater than your static. Trap his leg across your own and finish him.

Examples of Knee Pinch Passes

You'll arrive in new geography after a knee pinch pass than that for standard mounts, because your opponent may still have your would-be attacked leg clutched in his arm.

Be creative, but practice the basics of your top-half game. You'll find a great many transitions appear as you practice your knee pinch passes.

Shinbox Mount to Omoplata Roll

Once you pass your opponent's knee pinch, if he clutches your ankle desperately, he'll most likely continue to do so as you perform this roll. Continue sitting on his chest, but tuck your knee into his shoulder and over his biceps to block the far arm, keeping wrist control while you do so. (The photos on facing page illustrate this sequence.)

Lift his attacking elbow and drive your leg through, pointing your toes toward his head to enter what I call the shinbox mount.

Reach down with your near arm and grab your ankle. You'll need this grab so you can stuff it in your leg triangle as you roll.

In one motion, release his wrist and reach over your head toward the ground like you're about to perform a granby (a lateral roll across your shoulders.) This will shift your weight off the knee by his head.

1. Seated mount with your ankle attacked; get wrist control.

2. Grab top ankle with near arm, keeping wrist control.

3. Lift elbow to insert shinbox mount, keeping wrist control.

4. Granby roll.

5. Omoplata.

Immediately lace in your leg triangle, assisting with your near arm.

As you clear his chest, you'll begin to roll perpendicular to your initial lateral roll, so you'll be heading into *omoplata*. Finish in the standard manner or with any of the variations you already know. Omoplata details are outside the scope of this book, but you get the picture.

Shin Roll to Elbow Slice

If as you knee-pinch pass, he keeps both hands laced for the would-be leg attack so that you cannot sit fully in mount on his chest, with your knee up and foot flat on the mat, reach under your thigh and pin his attacking wrist to his chest with your near arm.

Step out of mount and to cross-side with your free leg. Continue to wind the knee of your attacked leg around, placing your shin into his biceps, knee flat on the mat. Point your toes!

Insert your hips on top of his forearm. Remember the rule of thirds: place the bottom third of your shin as deeply as possible into the bottom third of his upper arm (closest to his elbow). If he attempts to wiggle out, maintain wrist control so he can't escape.

If he's strong, under-hook and block his neck with your near arm and his near hip with your far arm.

Drive your hips down to finish. Avoid driving your shin back so you don't release the hold. Drive the blade of your shin beneath his biceps into his elbow pit to separate his elbow. Biceps crushes hurt like hell and cause bruises, but most fighters can tolerate them. However, elbow separations are a different story altogether, and they'll quickly tap or snap.

1. Standing mount while two arms attack one ankle; get wrist control.

2. Mount to cross-side, dropping knee.

3. Insert shin to slice; keep wrist control.

4. Maintain wrist control and under-hook his neck.

DOUBLE-KNEE PINCH

The double-knee pinch is the structurally weaker of the two pinches because positional control over the legs is virtually nonexistent. Outward pressure (abduction) is stronger than inward (adduction) physiologically, so your opponent can press your legs apart somewhat easily, unless you have developed significant attribute strength.

The double-knee pinch is not recommended, even if you have rolled your opponent onto his belly. I mention it here because in a scramble anyone can make mistakes, and even an advanced grappler can get caught.

The double-knee pinch does happen more often than you may think, such as from lower-half knee on diaphragm setting up the double-ankle lock.

Keeping his near knee pinched, lift up his far ankle off the mat with your far arm.

Drive your near arm over that lifted leg, getting the ankle buried underneath your armpit. Keep reaching down on the near side beyond his near ankle to trap his top leg.

Before you turn to your back, flex your arm back to your body so that his bottom ankle is blocked in your elbow pit. Make sure his shin blade aligns with the back of his top Achilles tendon.

Gable grip and finish him with a double-ankle submission.

1. Knee-on-diaphragm, double-ankle lock setup.

2. Double-knee pinch; pull upward on his left leg.

3. Reach through and secure opposite ankle.

4. Flex back to lock in double ankle submission.

CHAPTER 11

DEFENSES AGAINST THE SADDLE

To defend against the saddle positions, you must first be able to apply them. Once you can establish and maintain the position, you'll discover where you can "create slop" in your opponent's leg triangle; where you can establish wiggle room to regain lunar plexus, hip, and even knee control; and, as a result, where you can sweep and reverse him.

BREAKING THE TRIANGLE

Most defenses against the saddle involve breaking the triangle:

1. Unlace the over-lacing leg from between the sits bones. If it's tightly in place, bring your knees together and use your close arm in front of his ankle to scoop out his leg and begin unknotting his triangle.

1. Remove the hooked foot.

2. Press away his over-lacing leg.

3. Foot plant with knee control.

4. Wrist control.

2. Fire-pole down his over-laced leg so that you can free your thigh, knocking your opponent out of the saddle. If you compress him low enough, he won't have the leverage to apply any locks and will be forced to transition.

3. Plant your trapped leg's foot on the mat so that a lock cannot be applied. Obviously your opponent will be crocodile-rolling and hip-heisting to prevent this. While it's planted, you're temporarily stalemated.

4. Control his wrists so he can't finalize a lock. However, if you don't know how to control his wrists, you'll just burn energy while he relaxes in the saddle. You're using wrist control to minimize sweeps so that you can get to your feet, unknot his under-hooked leg, and pull to guard pass.

COUNTERATTACKS AGAINST THE SADDLE

By breaking the leg triangle, some saddle defenses are counterattacks themselves. Two of the basic saddle counterattacks are the paper-cutter calf crush and the double-ankle lock.

Paper-Cutter Calf Crush

Clear his over-lacing leg from under your sits bones to lessen danger to your attacked leg.

With your far arm, under-hook his ankle and, with your near-arm gable grip, place your forearm over his instep like a paper-cutter choke. You'll need to pinch your top elbow in toward your centerline to get it in place.

Pry down on his foot and lever up on your underside wrist into his calf.

This action is painful and causes bruises, but tougher fighters will be able to relax into it. Against stand-up strikers with super-tight calves, or people not used to leg attacks, this works like a charm.

1a and b. Clear the over-lacing leg to the outside.

2. Lock in gable grip.   **3. Pry down and lever up.**

Double-Ankle Lock

Clear his over-lacing leg from under your sits bones.

As he attempts to triangle over the top of your hips, reach under his under-laced heel with your near elbow to apply the double Achilles lock.

1a and b. Clear the over-lacing leg to the outside.

2a–c. Lace in the double-ankle lock.

Bow-and-Arrow Knee Compression

If you're saddled by your opponent, but are defending your attacked leg by placing your foot flat on the mat (thereby keeping him on his back with his knee off the mat), you can string the bow and arrow lock.

With your same side arm, help him bury his knee in the leg triangle deeply, threading your elbow underneath his ankle. If his triangle is very deep into the "rule of thirds" on his shin, you can turn the blade of his shin into his other knee. Lift as high as possible with the crook of your elbow. You can use your other hand in a gable grip for extra leverage. While pulling his ankle deep into his knee, scoot your sits bones to press his ankle toward his hips.

Wrap your under-lacing hand on the inside of his thigh and your other hand around the outside of his thigh and gable grip. Hug his thigh tightly while driving your butt into his ankle to cause the knee compression.

If you can roll to your side, you can throw your free leg over his thigh for additional compression.

This move is different from a calf crush, which, like the biceps crush, is painful and causes bruises, but not nearly as agonizing as the sinew-separating knee slice. If you are flexible enough and can get close enough, overhook your nonattacked leg over his thigh to increase the pressure. However, the bow and arrow doesn't work against people with loose knees, so gauge your opponent's flexibility before attempting it.

1. Foot flat on mat blocking full saddle.

2. Gable grip ankle; pull and scoot.

3. Hand-lace over his thigh and gable grip.

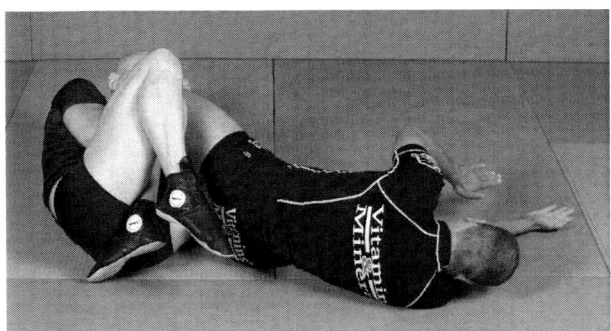

4. Roll to side and drive toward hip to hip.

5a and b. Over-lace your nonattacked leg.

Side Saddle Swirly Knee Compression

If your opponent has secured the side saddle on you, you still can defend yourself if you act before he can apply the tourniquet.

Reach up with your near arm and pull the inside of his knee on top of your attacked thigh. Pull it as high to your chest as possible as you fire-pole down and lock in your own leg triangle.

To keep your opponent from seeing this setup coming, you can fake the double-ankle submission so that he buries his leg triangle deep into his knee pit. It's not really a fake because if he allows you to finish him here, do it. No reason to be elaborate if step one ends it.

With your other arm, scoop the outside of his foot and grab your hands together on his foot.

Pull his ankle around in a spiral swirly toward his thigh to drive his own leg triangle deep into separating his knee.

While you pull his knee toward his thigh, apply the tourniquet to prevent his knee from being able to leak leverage.

1. Side-saddled.

2. Scoop his knee and fire pole down; leg triangle into full saddle.

3. Scoop his over-lacing ankle with your near arm and pull until you can grab with both hands.

4. Pull the knee around in a semicircle toward his thigh.

• • •

The above techniques are just the basics of countering the family of positions that I call the saddle. There are much more sophisticated reversals, sweeps, recounters, and escapes, but they won't make sense until you've mastered the basics covered in this book.

CHAPTER 12

BASIC SADDLE SWEEPS

Once you understand how to lock down the saddle through the fire pole, leg triangle, and tourniquet, you'll need to know how the opponent can move as he tries to escape.

You will eventually figure this out if you just lock down the saddle and have your opponent go live. But to save you some time, energy, and potential injury, let's discuss the basic sweeps that you'll need to know in order to maintain the positional dominance you've worked so hard to establish.

The three basic sweeps in the saddle are the shinbox sweep, crocodile roll, and windshield wiper.

SHINBOX SWEEP

Most often when you're in saddle, the opponent tries to pull up to top half, as if in half guard.

This attempt is like the shin rock escape from the knee pinch. However, with your shin in your opponent's hip fold, this is impossible. As he pulls up, press your shin deep into his hip fold as you elevate your hips.

At the same time, pop up the back of the elbow he's posting on the ground. If he's control-ling your wrists, perform a simple wrist release as you elevate him with your hips. If he has strong wrist control, remain calm and exhale. Even though he appears to be on top, you have positional dominance. He's burning major energy trying this, so let him waste himself. Just take your time and release his wrists.

Drive down your over-lacing leg toward the mat and then immediately make sure you secure that free foot in a secure position. Reset the full saddle knee to the floor.

2. Shin-press and elevate hips.

3. Elbow pop and wrist release.

1a–c. Pulls up to top-half.

4. Reset full saddle.

CROCODILE ROLL

This is not a common sweep against fighters who have an experienced lower-half game. Beginners, and even intermediate-level lower-half fighters, will try to roll to their bellies, thinking that doing so will reduce the leverage of your hold. But it has the opposite effect. It places your hip behind the lock and adds gravity to your advantage.

The crocodile roll involves your gluing to his roll and letting it happen. If he continues to roll to his back again, surf his roll and then reset the saddle more tightly.

When you get comfortable with the saddle, you'll be able to deepen your position as he rolls, growing tighter and tighter with each revolution: better leg triangle, deeper fire pole, tighter tourniquet. I strongly suggest you begin in this position and practice the roll often.

1a and b. He high-legs over to belly.

2. Full saddle on belly gravity submission.

3a and b. Reset the saddle.

WINDSHIELD WIPER

Sometimes the opponent will attempt to roll over and feel the danger of being crocodile-rolled. A common mistake for many fighters is to think that if they get to base, then they'll be safe even though you're still in the saddle.

Instead of rolling, he steps over to the outside, across your saddle, and goes to base on all fours.

Roll with him to your belly, maintaining the saddle, and extend your hips into the mat to finalize the lock.

However, if you do not finalize and he continues over to his base, as you extend your hips, extend your arms overhead and shrimp to the opposite direction, like a windshield wiper.

As he goes to base, shrimp up like you're pulling up the fire pole. This will load his hip for the sweep.

At the same time, continue the roll to your opposite side. At this point, press your shin into his hip fold and drive your over-lacing leg toward his trapped leg.

He'll fall right back into a reset of the saddle. Once you get comfortably strong with your saddle mechanics and the swim, you'll find that you can use it proactively to get deeper into the position. The third component of this sweep is actually a sweep from seated guard against a standing opponent.

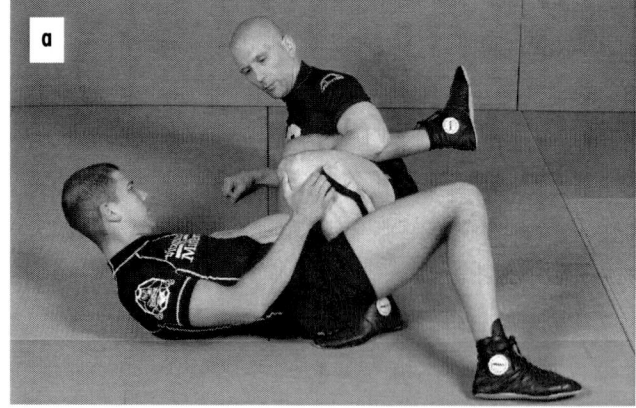

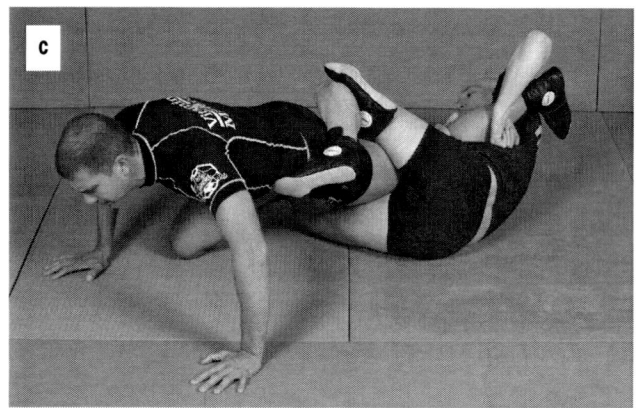

1a–c. He steps over saddle to base.

2. Crocodile to belly.

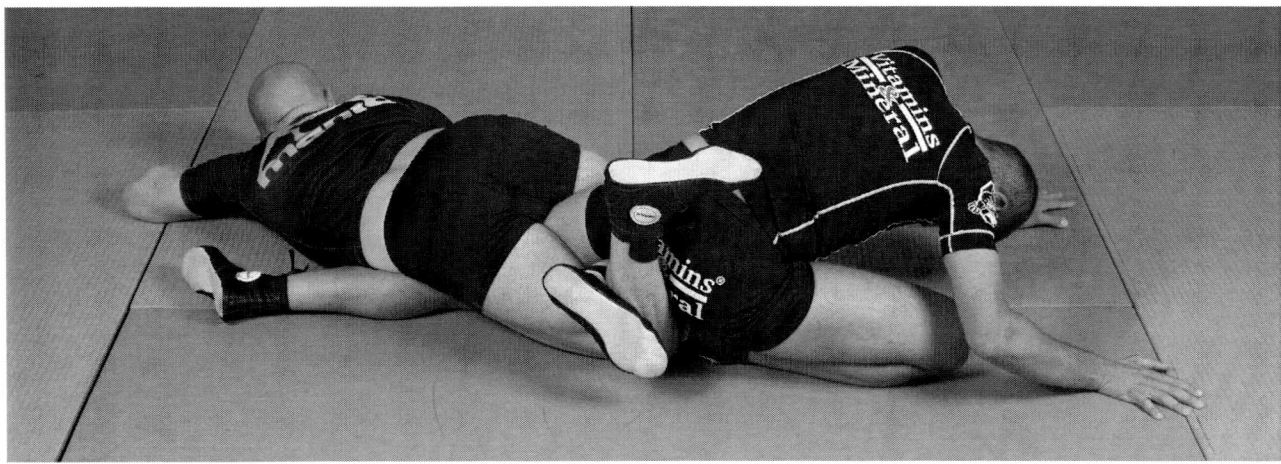

3. Swim around.

4. Shrimp back up.

5. Shin sweep back to saddle reset.

READY FOR THE SUBMISSIONS?

Having practiced the above, I do believe that you should consider practicing my variations on leg locks. My leg lock tactics are positionally based, requiring little strength as a result, but they demand that you be methodical in isolating and controlling your opponent's hips and attacked knee.

After a few years of practice, you'll find that you're nailing submissions with less and less structure due to the precision of your application. Don't be fooled by watching higher-ranked belts pulling off what appears to be "free-wrestling" submissions. Those subs *do* happen, but only because of developing precision through position. My records show that against competitors of equal experience and conditioning, you will only land free-wrestling/nonpositional submissions 20 percent of the time.

Focus on the basics. Practice only from, with, and through position. Then, thank God when you're given a "freebie" submission with little position.

CHAPTER 13

BASIC SUBMISSIONS IN SADDLE: POSITIONAL LEG LOCKS

Fast-wrestling to leg locks has been adopted by even good jiujitsu fighters (who should know better), but it's mostly been because people have assumed—since some sambo fighters are able to land a fortunate 20 percent of leg locks without first establishing stable position (the saddle)—that leg locks can only be landed by fast-wrestling. However, that's just not the case. You can substantially increase the percentage of successful attempts, the painful depth of application, the safety of staying in (saddle) position without being swept from your failed attempt, and the vast technical options that become open to you.

PROXIMODISTAL STRATEGY:
LOCKING FROM POSITION TO SUBMISSION

Proximodistal means that you're first securing control over the most central point—his core or "lunar plexus"—and then working joint by joint out to the end of his leg: from core to pelvis to hip to knee and finally to ankle.

Notice in the following examples how the knee pushes into the ribs as the hips drive forward to lengthen away from the opponent's body. Note how your arms remain tight and protected, not going for the submission until you've secured the knee and, finally, the ankle and foot. A good saddle should *always* progress in this fashion: control his breath by knee position in ribs, thigh down; control his hips by the tourniquet effect of your leg triangle; secure his knee as you lengthen away; and, only at the end, wrap the ankle to finalize the submission.

THE SEVEN CORE LEG LOCKS
IN THE SADDLE

The following seven submissions have many variations and many exotic applications. However, as a coach, I've had to come up with the simplest format for teaching them. You could spend a lifetime just refining your leg attacks. However, leg locks are only one aspect of the lower-half game, which is only one half of the ground game, which is only a fraction of a total fight. So what I have worked vigorously at developing over the years is a syllabus of core skills, which, if studied, would hammer in the primary mechanics and foster creativity during actual fighting.

By focusing on these seven core locks, you will find that you have a significantly higher percentage of success with leg attacks than if you were to allot your already limited time to much more random, lower-percentage attacks. You will also discover that by practicing these locks, specifically from the saddle positions, that you will be able to create new applications spontaneously without actually having to necessarily practice the new techniques.

Most of the holds are a kinetic, or flow, chain connected by a maneuver I created called the back brace. The back brace came about because I needed to use my hands to fight off wrist control while isolating the attacked leg with my elbows and shoulders, as well as maintaining positional dominance using my hands as posts or braces. You'll find that the back brace quickly becomes one of the most crucial components of your leg finishes.

Back brace.

The back brace isolation is the setup movement for the Achilles, ankle, or heel lock. Tuck your elbow behind your back and place your hand on your bottom, pinching your arm to

your ribs. Keep the back brace snug as the opponent rolls or squirms, because when the submission appears, you'll be able to finish quickly without "speeding" or moving rapidly.

The slower you move, the better your hold will be, which in turn increases your chances of success. This is why I teach locks from the position outward: lunar plexus to hip to knee to ankle. The back brace will be an essential component in increasing your success percentage.

1. Achilles Lock

Achilles Lock.

Probably the most misunderstood leg lock is the one that should actually be practiced first and most often: the Achilles lock. One of the best ways to train in this technique is to have it applied to you. This is more than just gaining a kinesthetic awareness of the sweet spot. Unlike with joint locks, repeated exposure diminishes the impact; like a form of deep massage.

I'm a stickler for nuance and could damn near write a book just on the minutiae of this lock, but the truth is that having the right technique (which is rare) is insufficient. You do need to drill and drill and drill it until you own it. Once you own it, you will slap it on anywhere and everywhere.

Please take the time to go through this section—resist the temptation to think you know how to do an Achilles just fine and skip ahead to the cool sweeps. This is the real magic right here.

The rule of thirds means that you must apply the bottom third of your forearm as the

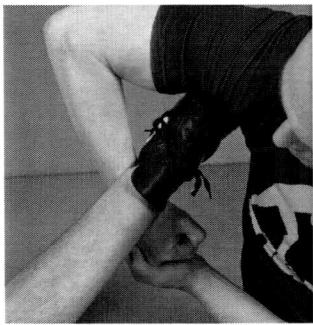

One-third forearm, one-third lower leg.

fulcrum against the bottom third of your opponent's lower leg: in particular, the top (distal) end of your radius bone in the nook above his heel (the calcaneus bone that juts out and forms the heel). Most fighters overcommit their forearms and apply soft tissue against soft tissue. Even the strongest man in the world, at the wrong place, will not be able to elicit pain.

The fulcrum of this lock must be directly perpendicular to the Achilles. Think of applying your forearm as a blade to cut the tendon. Most fighters neglect to keep this perpendicular fulcrum as they try to apply strength. However, the more that you maintain a right angle to your opponent's Achilles, the less force you need.

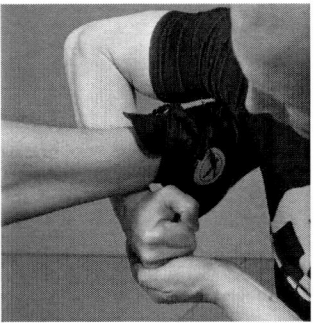

Get perp with blade.

Leg Slide

To secure thirds on the Achilles, slide back with your over-hooking arm until you snag snugly with your radius in place at the butt of his heel. It's best to practice this slowly with your forearm perpendicular to his lower leg until you find the right spot.

Choke back to heel.

Elbow Tuck

Once you become comfortable with being perpendicular, you can begin to tuck in your elbow to your ribs, removing all space from the lock. This changes the angle of the fulcrum and, as a

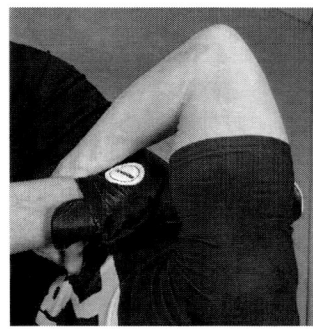

Tuck elbow.

result, makes a smaller surface. Although you may see successful fighters tucking in their elbows, if you're just starting out, don't practice that way. You'll struggle unsuccessfully for years. Start perpendicular until you nail it consistently against resistance and then slowly start tucking in the elbow.

Wrist Scoop

Once you slide into place, some fighters will instinctively pull their toes toward their shin and drive their heels away. This extends the calf muscle and strengthens the tendon, making it more difficult to apply the lock. The scoop is the action of rotating your wrist toward his heel, applying pressure, and then continuing to rotate your wrist back to perpendicular. This allows you to soften his tendon and reapply the lock.

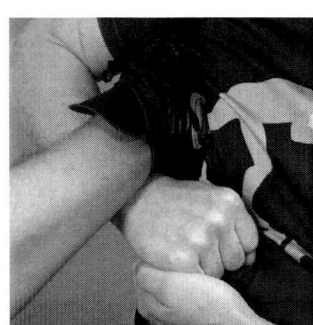

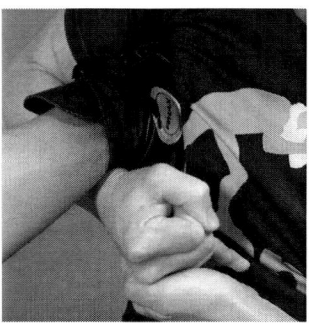

Scoop toward and then away.

Shoulder Roll

As you scoop and tuck, roll your applying shoulder back before leaning at all with your torso. Most fighters will overzealously attempt to apply more force by laying down their backs. However, the shoulder roll will be sufficient force for most opponents to submit. As you roll your shoulder back, it will tuck your elbow deeper toward your hip, and allow you to lift the wrist fulcrum higher and harder into his Achilles.

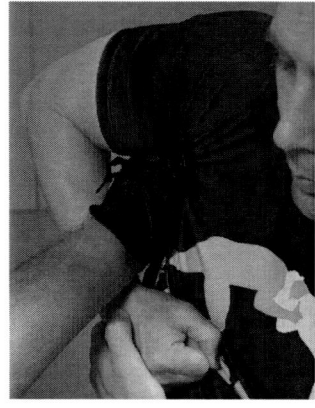
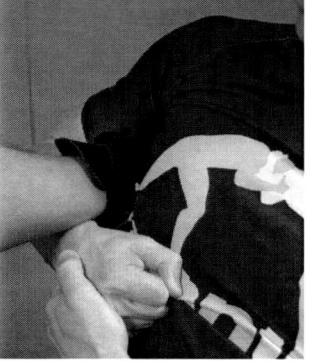

Roll shoulder.

Fist in Pelvis Hip Drive

I won't expand too much on the squeeze here. If you've been practicing your tourniquet, you're ready to go. You need the tourniquet so that you can apply your hip drive. If you don't apply the tourniquet, then the knee will leak force as you apply the wrist fulcrum and the shoulder downward.

Most fighters neglect to realize that a lever has three forces: the wrist fulcrum, armpit lock, and tourniquet squeeze with the hip drive. Squeezing on the tourniquet will allow you to maximize how much of the force you're applying to your opponent's Achilles to translate into pain. It will also

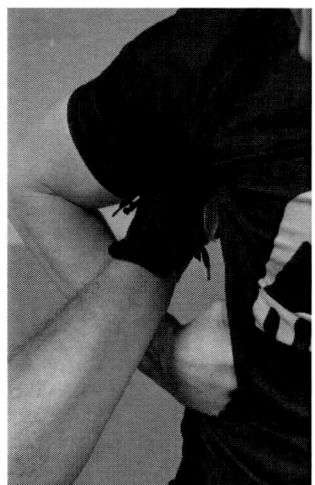

Fist in pelvis for hip drive.

allow you to lift your hips to drive his thigh away, locking his knee in place and maximizing the lever. If you can roll to your belly, you'll be able to add gravity behind your lock and really turn on the juice.

The Pulse

Because this is a painful soft-tissue hold, it's important to understand some of the geek stuff underpinning why it works and when it doesn't. The brain only allows this kind of pain to be sustained for about 47 seconds; obviously, that's an eternity in grappling. However, since the duration slowly diminishes the pain, like a dimmer switch (rather than a total shut-off like a toggle switch), the pulse actually increases the pain. The pulse really isn't an independent mechanical move, but more of a method of application. Apply pressure in short bursts and let off (but don't release the mechanics).

2. Ankle Lock

Although most fighters try to learn the ankle lock before the Achilles, the ankle lock follows an Achilles attack tactically and physiologically. I don't place as much emphasis on the ankle as I do on the Achilles, because if you learn a good Achilles lock, the ankle lock will happen just from good mechanics. However, the reverse is not true.

Learning how to do an ankle lock will not give you a good Achilles lock. There are details in the ankle lock that you will only discover by practicing the Achilles. You cannot get them from practicing the ankle lock alone, since the Achilles lock precedes the ankle both tactically (in when you apply them) and physiologically (in how you apply them).

The ankle lock is actually the hyperextension of the foot. So, unlike with the Achilles, where his foot's geography isn't essential, you must roll back your shoulder to extend his toe point. All the lever details of the ankle lock are the same as for the Achilles, except for the fact that the shoulder roll must drive his foot and toes down to point where his foot is in line with his shin. You must maintain a right angle of your wrist to his Achilles.

Shoulder roll to toe point.

Reread and reapply the nuances of the Achilles lock to finalize the ankle lock. Your radial bone now separates the top of his ankle joint due to the hyperextended position and application of the fulcrum underneath.

3. Heel Hook

Most fighters mistake the heel hook for a foot attack. It is a knee attack to cause submission, through the threat of tearing ligaments. It is the most dangerous weapon in the leg attack arsenal, and it should be taught last for that reason.

Only a mature fighter should be permitted to use heel hooks because there is little pain in the heel hook until it's too late. It's not like an Achilles lock where the pain causes the submis-

Back brace.

sion. When a fighter is prepared to give up the heel hook to prevent his opponent from having his knees permanently hobbled, then he's ready to add this finishing hold to his repertoire.

The heel hook is set up most effectively by

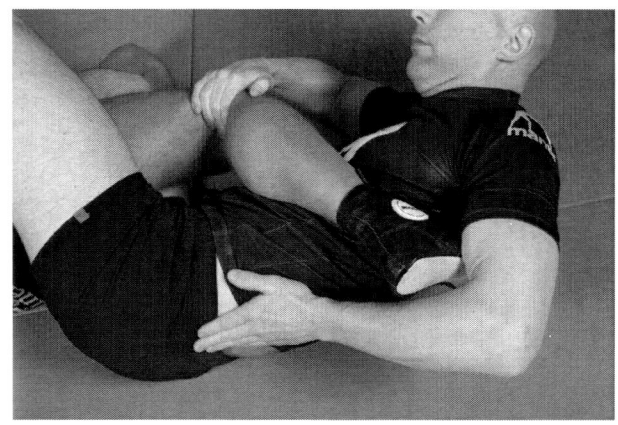

Heel pop.

blocking an opponent's lower leg with the back brace. As he rolls to avoid the back brace, or to counter the Achilles or the ankle lock, he will force his own heel to pop out of your elbow nook.

Optimally, you want this to happen when you have bumped his lower leg across to the shoulder opposite your saddle. However, you can land the heel hook from the same side.

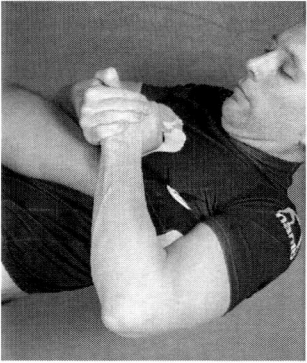

Gable grip.

Gable-grip to lock in the heel and prepare for the corkscrew finish— my favorite variation that I created for competition.

The heel hook can be either internal or external.

Internal Heel Hook

In the internal heel hook, the outside of the opponent's heel is exposed from your elbow nook, and the outside edge or "foot-sword" is buried into your armpit.

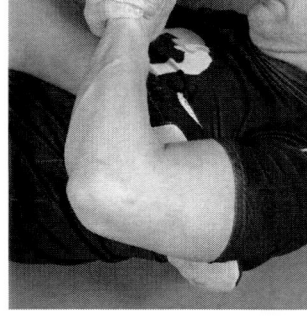

Internal heel hook.

External Heel Hook

In contrast, in the external heel hook, the inside of the opponent's heel is exposed from your elbow nook, and the inside edge or "instep" is buried into your armpit.

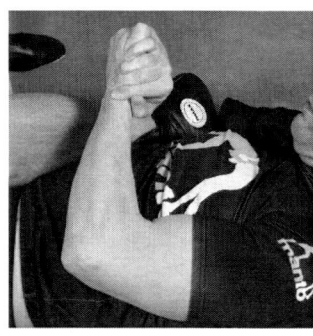

External heel hook.

Corkscrew

The corkscrew heel hook is the most effective (highest percentage), most efficient (greatest results for the least energy investment), and most dangerous (chance of injury due to small range of motion). I call it the corkscrew because it has two complementary and opposite motions: a push down on the top third of the opponent's foot, and a pull up on the bottom third of his foot. Also, you push and pull around a point of rotation, like the handle of a corkscrew. Executing a corkscrew is different than loosening a jar lid. A jar lid stays in place as you turn it (mostly.) A corkscrew increases in height as you turn it.

The point of rotation for both hooks is the middle of the opponent's foot. That means the two ends of the lever must move to maximize the efficiency of the lock. Most fighters over-muscle the heel hook by trying to rip the heel upward around the point where the opponent's foot is trapped. It can work, but it has a much lower percentage of success and has an increased chance of the opponent escaping.

The two complementary and opposite motions happen as follows:

- Perform the shoulder roll just like you would in the Achilles lock to drive his toes downward.
- Simultaneously, with your forearm in the nook behind your opponent's calcaneus, and in a gable grip, drive your elbow

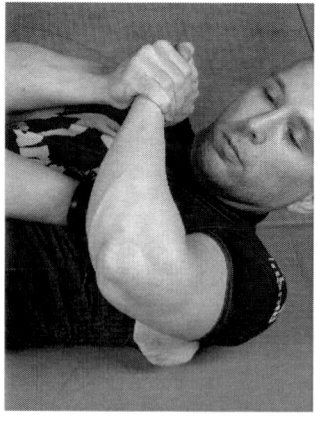

Corkscrew.

forward first, while pulling your gable grip up in a circle toward the far side of your neck.

These two complementary forces create a very tight, very short-range, very quickly finalized lock. Even if you've done heel hooks for years, this variation is extremely dangerous and much faster than any you've done before unless you've been training in it already (and if you have, then you know to go slowly).

The tourniquet is absolutely the most important element of the heel hook, as it prevents the thigh from moving to leak leverage on the hold. The tighter your tourniquet, the more the soft tissue inside his knee isolates the strain. Once you feel the leg and hip drive in the tourniquet, you'll feel where you're actually separating the sinews of his knee before you even begin the corkscrew.

4. Foot Lock

The strongest and most effective foot lock, called inversion, moves the foot inward medially, as if you were overtreading your ankle on high-soled shoes. An eversion foot lock is possible, but it is much harder to learn and has a lower percentage of success compared to refining the inversion lock.

Most often fighters make the mistake of letting the knee leak leverage by keeping the knee bent and not keeping the leg fully in contact with the opponent's torso.

The rule of thirds still applies here. In your

1. Secure knee.

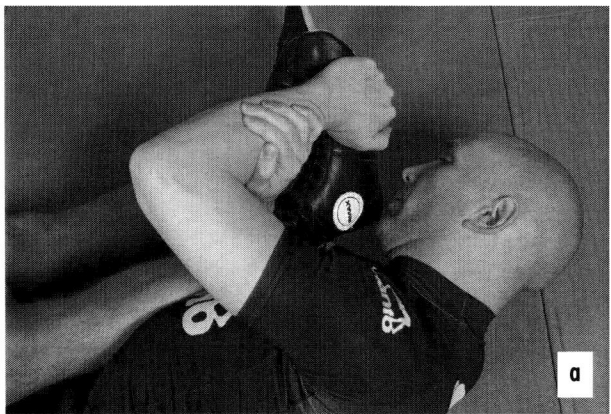

a

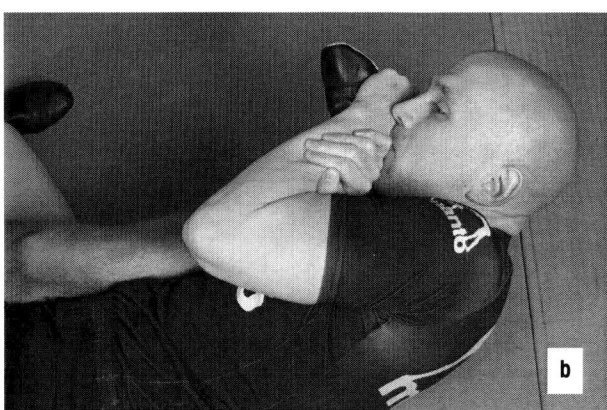

b

4a and b. Chest curl.

arm triangle, bring the bottom third of your forearm (your wrist) to the bottom third of the opponent's ankle. Grab the bottom third of your other wrist. Although you could get it with a higher grip on your forearms, the energy required to cause submission is much greater, it takes greater range of motion to cause submission, and there is longer time for escape.

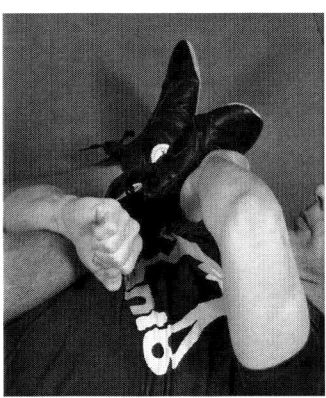

2. Tight thirds.

The Achilles lock lessons still apply even in the foot lock. Pinch your elbows to your ribs, forearms to your chest, and scoop your wrist (radial bone) into the nook of the inside of his ankle.

While you scoop, hug his foot with your chest and perform a spinal crunch to cause his ankle inversion.

You certainly can do this free of your body, but the pain is so much greater, the range of motion so much smaller, and the chance of escape so much less likely when your hold is snug.

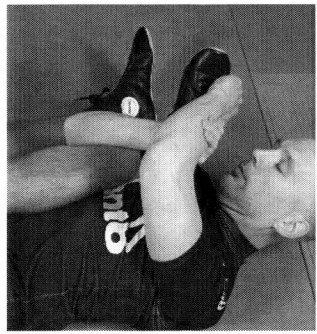

3. Scoop to nook.

5. Double Achilles

Although this may appear to be an exotic lock, because it involves two legs and can be reduced to a more basic lock within its mechanics, it's absolutely a high-percentage move. As a result, it is a core technique for your repertoire.

The opponent's bottom leg is on the outside and his top on the inside. When you see this geography, make sure that you shoot your primary arm as deeply as possible.

Once your elbow pit clears his heel, flex your forearm back to sink your elbow behind his Achilles,

1. Shoot the arm deeply.

2. Flex the arm back.

snugly in the nook above his heel. His top foot will be buried in your armpit as if performing an ankle lock (which you sometimes nail on top of the double Achilles).

Lace in a gable grip for your leverage, and hug your forearms to your chest and ribs at a right angle to prevent escape.

The rule of thirds applies once again. You will use the bottom third of your opponent's shin against the bottom third of his other lower leg: his Achilles.

Fighters often make the mistake of not pulling in the proper direction and will instead substitute greater strength for precision. Pull your gable grip so that you're curling your under-lacing arm from fist to opposite shoulder. Keep your elbows tucked in as you do so.

Think of his shinbone as a sword. If you don't shoot your arm through far enough to bury his

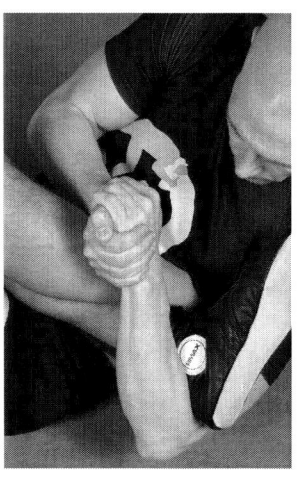

3. Lace the gable grip.

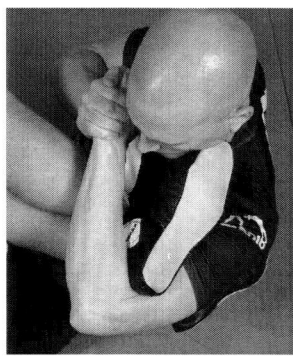

4. Curl to opposite shoulder.

heel nook into your elbow pit, you will be shallow. That means that when you lever his bottom leg into his Achilles, it will be the flat of the sword, the inside or medial plane of the tibia—his shin. Feel your shin. Feel where that sword edge is on the top and where it slides flat to the inside. You want to pull that sword edge into his Achilles. It causes enormous pain when you do, and only minor pain when you pull the flat of the sword.

You also need to ensure that the tourniquet is on tightly so that he cannot twist his trapped, attacked Achilles away from the sword edge.

I also perform

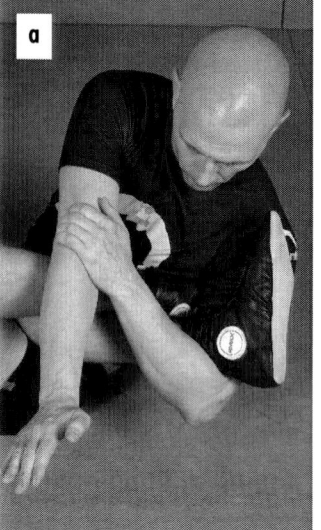

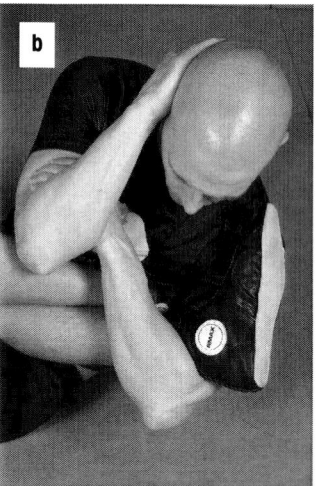

5a and b. Double-ankle submission variation.

another variation using an arm triangle secured behind my neck to finish the double-ankle submission.

6. Knee Bar

I've finished many of my fights with the knee bar mechanics you'll learn here. It's not the only way. There are many exotic knee bars, especially in traditional sport sambo, but these mechanics are high percentage for MMA—the focus of this book.

The knee bar is one of the most misunderstood finishing holds because people look at the knee as analogous to the elbow. Due to the density of muscle and connective tissue, and the stabilization it creates to resist mobility in order to maintain upright posture against gravity, the knee requires much more sophisticated nuance to finalize in submission.

Although the mechanics of arm bar attacks do not transfer directly over to attacks on the knee, the reverse is not true. If you practice these nuances, you will find that your arm bar attacks will end much more quickly, with much tighter application decreasing the chance of escape, and with a higher percentage of success.

There is only one knee bar that you should practice and drill. All others will be improvised by internalizing the corkscrew that you developed in the heel hook. In the knee bar, the corkscrew action is smaller. You should develop your heel hook first so you understand the effect that it has on the knee.

As the name suggests, there are two force applications: pulling the knee apart to lengthen the tissues before applying the leverage to the knee, and pulling the knee in a spiral action to lock tight the tissue to prevent flexibility from reducing your success.

Think about the way your knee works. It doesn't deliberately rotate, because it needs to be stable to hold you upright and move you

forward. As a result, twisting the knee (much like a heel hook) helps accelerate how fast you can finish the hold. Don't worry; it doesn't take much of a twist. The knee works best when compressed. When you separate it, the tissues are already tight before you even begin to apply force.

I suggest practicing the knee bar from the reverse saddle, beginning with your opponent's knee bent. Cinch up the fire pole, apply the tourniquet, and hug his thigh to your body.

Bend over his knee with your chest, and take the back of your hand to scoop up the underside of his heel.

Move your hand behind your ear to lengthen out his knee. But as you do, keep his shin on your chest and use your body to extend, rather than merely pull with your arm. Inflexible fighters will tap even this far into the hold.

Take your opposite hand across your other and grab his Achilles behind the nook of his calcaneus. Pinch your elbows together, with your forearms married to his lower leg. Tuck your head and place your initial hand behind your neck and head.

Cinch in deeper toward his hip and pulse on the tourniquet as tightly as possible before you insert your hips into his knee. This lockdown is a critical final step; if you don't

1. Reverse saddle with knee bent.

2. Back-of-hand scoop.

perform it, he may be able to leak leverage at his hips and turn his knee out of the way. The tourniquet—and the geography of the leg triangle immobilizing his hip—will prevent his escape.

You're not pressing your hips down as much as you're pulling his heel upward while driving his hips away with your leg triangle to extend your spine straight. Yes, that inserts your hips deeply, but it keeps the lock very tight with no air between his upper leg and your lower body, and between his lower leg and your torso. His knee separates before your hips start driving into it, causing enormous pain.

Once you feel comfortable with this body-extension technique, you'll want to start practicing the spiral force of the corkscrew: the action of pulling and twisting at the same time in two opposing motions. This torsion creates a "shear center" where the wound tissues experience great strain before you even begin to apply the force to your opponent's knee with your hips.

As you perform the body extension, rotate underneath the elbow of the arm grabbing his heel and rotate your entire torso. Simultaneously, drive the over-lacing leg of your saddle down and away in the opposite spiral. This will insert the hip of that leg into the knee bar rather than both hips.

The corkscrew is the most challenging nuance of the knee bar to learn, but has the greatest transfer to all other techniques, the greatest percentage chance of success, the least chance of escape, and the fastest rate of submission.

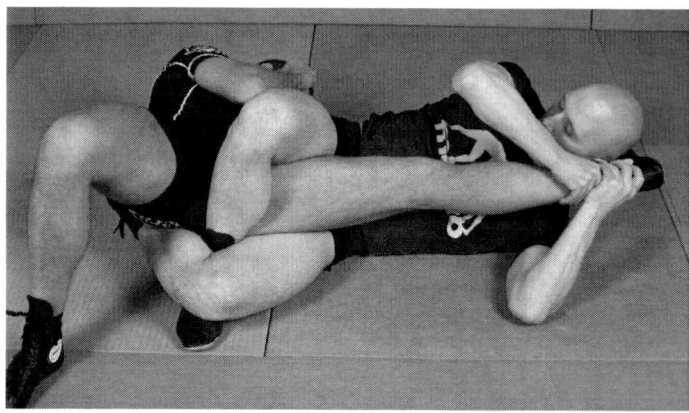

4. Hook with other hand and tuck.

3a and b. Move your hand behind your head and drive his body away.

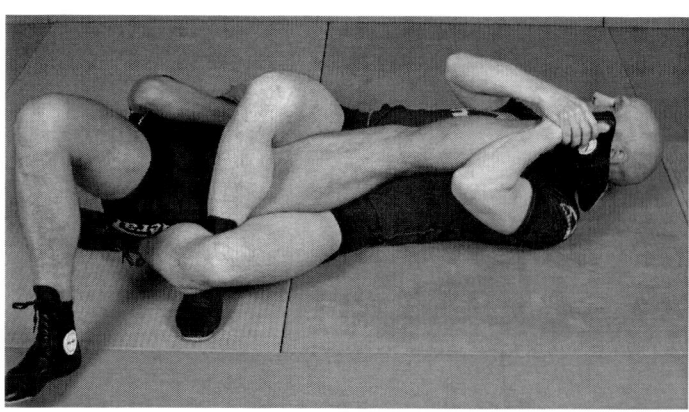

5. Pull up and push away.

7. Knee Slice

The knee slice, or compression, should be learned in conjunction with the knee bar. The variation that I coach is based on the reverse saddle holding position, though there are many variations. Also, I'm more concerned about the arm as the fulcrum in the slice than the leg. The leg fulcrum is a lower percentage move and more difficult to learn and apply, though it does happen and should not be ruled out. I have also found that if you practice the elbow fulcrum knee slice, you'll be able to understand the mechanics and improvise other fulcrums, including your opponent's leg and arm.

The rule of thirds applies as usual. You must insert the sword blade of your wrist's radius bone as deeply into his knee pit as possible. Most fighters sink in their fleshy forearm, thinking a larger fulcrum is better. That's not exactly correct. The deeper the fulcrum, the better.

While in a saddle, bury your wrist as deep as possible with your thumb up, pointed toward

1. Reverse saddle with knee bent.

2. Insert wrist.

3. Sink in arm triangle.

4. Lace over his leg.

5. Lace in your leg triangle.

his knee. Place the pinkie finger sword of your hand in your opposite elbow pit. Pull up with your elbow-pit as deeply as possible.

Most often you get into this position when your opponent is blocking you from the knee bar by crossing his legs in the opposite direction: non-saddled leg crossed over saddle leg. Since his leg is crossed, release your saddle and place your near leg (the same as the fulcrum arm) over the top of his crossed ankles. Lock in your leg triangle again.Roll your fulcrum-arm side of your body to the mat. Pull up and triangle your legs back to bring his heels to his sits bones to finish.

6. Roll to your side to finish.

7. Show crossed-leg block.

CHAPTER 14

GROUND ENTRIES FOR SADDLE

Once you understand how to establish the riding control of the saddle, you can begin to practice it in your tactical options during your groundfighting and standing grappling.

Unlike with traditional sambo, I believe that learning how to enter and transition into and out of the saddle positions from the ground takes priority over stand-up grappling entries. To my knowledge, this is a unique perspective, because traditional sambo holds the belief that if you perfect your throws, you will always land in the dominant position.

However, the reality of mixed martial arts competitions is that opponents don't always move the way you expect them to move. As a coach and athlete, I don't advise relying on perfect throws. Develop your groundfighting game and build, literally, from the ground up.

My unique "groundfighting" sambo approach will accelerate your submission fighting game because you can instantly incorporate it into your overall grappling strategy. It should be viewed as one of your options, not as a different strategy.

Imagine that the family of positions known as the "guard" were absent from jiujitsu. What would jiujitsu be like then? Just visualize it for a minute. Now, add the "guard" back into it. Think of how magnificent it is now, how contiguous and flowing.

Like the magnificence of adding the guard position back into jiujitsu, adding the "saddle" family of positions into your groundfighting game will expand your options dramatically, make your overall game much tighter and seamless—and completely baffle your opponents because you're fighting in a completely different way. Even opponents who know how to apply leg locks won't be able to understand how you're dismantling their attempts, while systematically executing your own.

I do believe that my approach to sambo—the sophistication of a positional "saddle" groundfighting strategy—is superior to traditional sambo. When you practice these skills, you can decide this for yourself.

CHAPTER 15

BASIC GUARD SERIES

SHINBOX ENTRY FROM OPEN GUARD

The shinbox entry was the first technique I ever created to enter the saddle against jiujitsu fighters because I had no training (or desire) to pass the guard. All my primary attacks were against the legs, so I really had no desire to leave the legs.

Standing versus open guard.

It's important, however, to understand what a good jiujitsu player considers here: what his goals are with his guard, the dangers of the triangle, *kimura,* and arm-bar, not to mention all of his sweeps from the guard. Once you do, your movement into this saddle entry will be a lot tighter and will have a higher percentage of success. It was really at this point that I began to see clearly the need to study jiujitsu in order to understand attacks from the guard.

The shinbox entry is the most important to know and develop because you will land it most frequently until your opponent develops a good saddle defense, which takes about one to two years of sustained practice.

Grab your opponent's ankles from underneath to control his hips. Typical top-half ground fighters expect you to try to pass by throwing his legs to one side, but you're not going to do that. Instead, lean toward his guard, but bring one of his heels to your centerline.

When first learning the shinbox entry, you'll need to practice isolating the attacked leg. Once you learn the move, you won't need to do this step any longer. Attacking the leg at your centerline, carefully step outside leg flat to the

mat. If you step too far, he'll scoop your far ankle and try to sweep, so keep your knee forward and ankle away from his reach. He doesn't feel in danger at this point since you're not trying to pass his guard, so he doesn't usually scramble. Just take your time and practice.

Drive forward off your back leg, while lifting your front shin and placing it across his hip fold. Lean your weight toward his far shoulder, and sink your shin in deeply while loading his diaphragm. At the same time, block his near shoulder under his armpit with your hand, and place your over-lacing knee toward the ground.

When you feel you can go no farther toward his far shoulder, start circling your weight toward his near shoulder. As your weight pins his near shoulder, lift your blocking arm and scoop under the knee you are attacking to fire-pole down.

Drop down to your side as you do so, to get your knee down to the mat, and begin to finalize the leg triangle.

If you focus on practicing this basic entry, most others become much easier and you'll more quickly wrap your head around the saddle game.

1. Lace over trapped leg.

2. Circle weight to near shoulder; scoop attacked knee.

3. Drop to your side and insert knee to his ribs; back brace.

4. Lock in leg triangle; tourniquet.

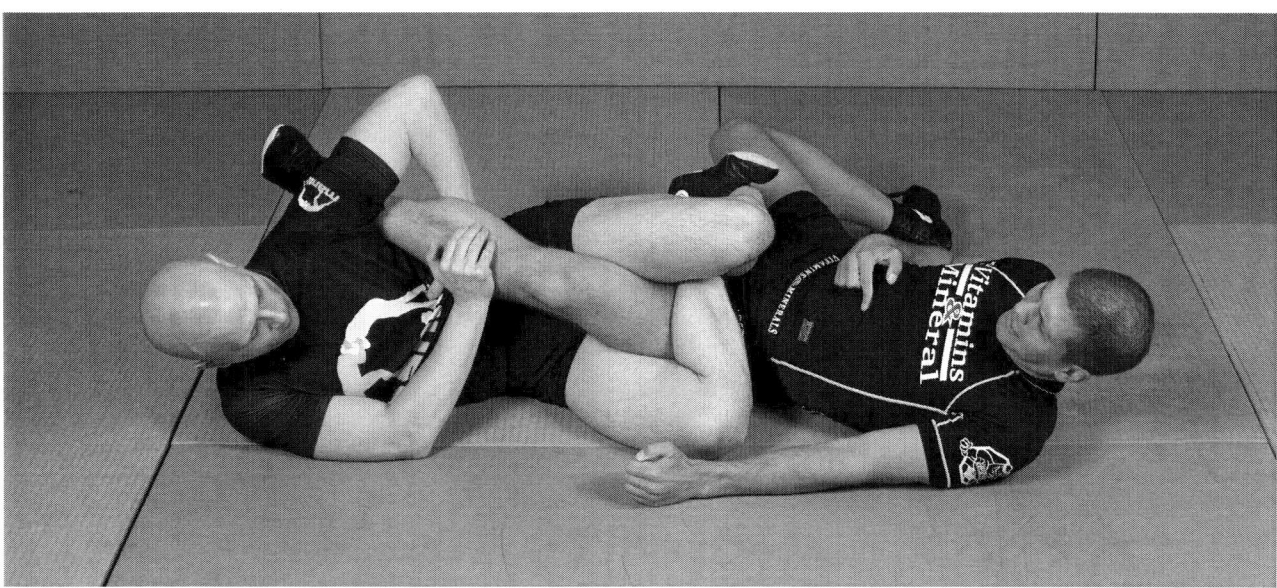

5. Finish with an Achilles lock.

THIGH-RIDE GUARD PASS

This type of guard pass developed out of the shinbox entry to the saddle, because it is also a basic guard pass in jiujitsu. Once you understand how to smear the leg across and start moving to cross-side, you'll start to feel when your opponent tries to shrimp away for half-guard, or get a knee between you, to get you back in his guard.

Scuttle close to his open guard and trap one leg, isolating his thigh with your knee and his foot in your armpit.

As he scoots to the side to hook your far leg, maintain control of the trapped leg. Place your knee over the thigh of his other leg.

Insert your top leg into his hip fold. Once you do, don't spin as much as you do in the shinbox, because you'll fall belly down. If you do, immediately move into the basic windshield wiper sweep.

Your knee drops immediately into position on the mat and in his ribs. Then you move on to the process of lacing in the leg triangle, tourniquet, and eventually the lock.

When you get smooth at this entry, you can start to make your opponent feel really uncomfortable about knowing which game you're going to use as you're passing his guard: top half or bottom half. It's all about how much you develop both your top-half and your lower-half groundfighting strategies. Sewn seamlessly together, they're ominous.

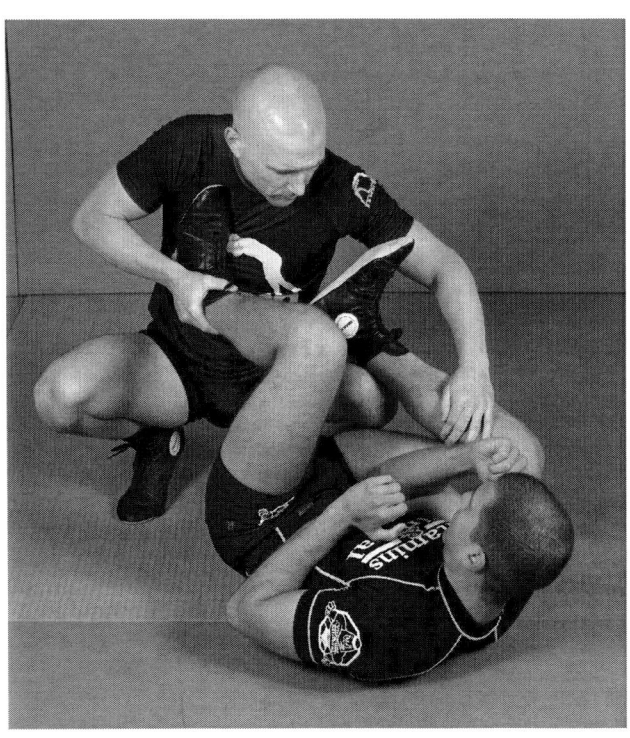

1. Trap his leg.

2. Block other thigh.

3. Grab your ankle and insert your shin to his hip fold.

4. Place your knee on the ground, switch hands, and crank in your leg triangle.

5. Lace in triangle; back brace.

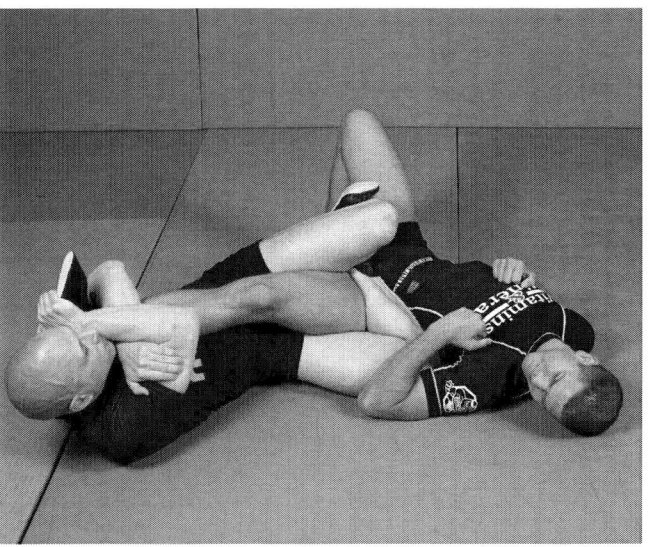

6. Finish with a foot lock.

REAR SHIN SWING VERSUS SEATED GUARD

This entry was actually created by sambo and jiujitsu fighter Wasakazu Imanari. He submitted most of his opponents so quickly that he never had to use a saddle to lock down the position. That may work well for lighter fighters, but for larger fighters like myself, facing much stronger opponents, I had to convert it to a saddle entry rather than the rolling knee-bar or rolling heel hook that Imanari would land.

As you approach your opponent in a shin squat, aim your flat foot leg in the middle of his seated guard. Now you can perform this as a nonclinch spin if you perform it quickly and smoothly (and luckily), but I suggest getting a whizzer over-hook on the arm in the direction you'll spin. Once you do, pull on his triceps to spin your back shin around parallel with the ground while on the ball of your front foot.

Lift your sits bones high enough to clear his knee, but no higher, because once you do clear his knee, sit down toward his hips.

At the same time, use your opposite arm to under-hook his knee and fire-pole as high as possible toward his hip.

When you can go no farther, start screwing your inserted leg from between his legs, to knee on the floor and shin in his hip fold.

Continue to fight with knee control until you can secure the leg triangle and begin the tourniquet.

It's a smooth entry that happens often. Often your opponent thinks that he's being given back position. There's a variation I'll show later that actually starts from bottom turtle, much like this.

1. Shin squat versus seated guard.

2. Get whizzer and begin spin.

3. Clear knee and sit down toward his hips.

4. Scoop knee and fire-pole.

5. Counterscrew over-lacing knee down.

6. Leg triangle, tourniquet; finish with heel hook.

THE WASHBURN:
JUMPING SEATED SPIN TO SADDLE AGAINST BUTTERFLY SCOOT

This technique earned its name from one of my athletes, Rob Washburn, a Washington State wrestling champ and jiujitsu fighter from Hawaii, who created it in class and began nailing it against everyone and anyone with whom he rolled. He slapped it on me for the first time, and my eyes went wide because no one had ever landed the saddle on me before. I was hugely surprised, impressed, and proud!

You face an opponent who butt-scoots in with the outside of one leg down on the mat and the other foot flat on the floor. Jumping into the saddle is much like the slow and controlled reverse shin swing. However, to jump, you need to clear the knee of the leg you intend to attack. To clear the knee, as you approach your opponent,

place flat on the ground the foot of the leg you're going to place in his hip fold—the top of your figure-4, which you'll be under-lacing into the leg triangle. Basically, this will always be your leg that is on the inside of your opponent's guard.

Push off your shin and shift your weight to the ball of your foot on the mat. Knee through and start the spin. Drive off the ball of your foot to jump back to his belly. Jump as deeply into him as possible to clear his knee. Sit down on his thigh, with your knee up. Don't lean back; lean forward and immediately scoop his knee with your outside arm.

Continue to spin your sits bones all the way around his thigh until you land your knee on the mat and in his ribs. Then continue to work the leg triangle in while getting your back brace ready to finalize the submission.

As you get comfortable with it, you can do this off the Prasara body-flow squat creep.

1. Triangle squat versus half-seated guard.

2a–c. Jump-spin back to belly with knee up; scoop his knee.

3a–c. Counterscrew knee down, leg triangle; finish with knee bar.

FLYING SADDLE VERSUS SCISSORS GUARD

You can hit the flying saddle pretty often if you practice from on the ground. If you learn to lock it on without very much distance to fall, you can get it much easier from standing, such as from a single leg takedown or ankle pick.

As you scoop your opponent's leg from a seated position, he inserts his other leg for a "scissors" half-guard.

Block him from spinning underneath to hook your far knee, by sitting down. You can also prevent him from spinning under by blocking his bottom thigh with your far hand, so he can't bend his knee and shrimp toward you.

Step up your far leg into a shin squat on the same side of the leg that you're attacking. Over-hook his bottom knee with the foot of your shin down the leg to continue to block his half guard.

Push off his thigh with your far hand and off your back shin as you step up and over the leg you've trapped. Push and press in the direction of his near shoulder—the same one as the attacked leg. Insert your shin in his hip fold.

As you place your shin in your opponent's hip fold and your knee on the ground, scoop up his opposite leg with your foot as you shift to your flat foot on the mat. Keep your shin blocking his opposite leg. To make sure you can continue to block this way, I suggest reaching up and using the crank to get your leg triangle on.

After a lot of practice, you'll eventually be able to land the flying saddle before you even hit the ground.

1. Scissors half-guard versus trapped leg seated guard.

2. Block his under-side leg.

3. Step to shin squat.

4. Push off thigh, press off shin, and insert shin to hip fold.

5. Knee-down and scoop his far knee up to block his leg.

6. Crank in leg triangle; fight knee down to mat.

7. Finish with heel hook.

BASIC KNEE-RIDE SERIES

COSSACK KNEE SWITCH TO
BOTTOM-SIDE KNEE RIDE

Switching from knee-on-belly (or, as I prefer, knee-on-diaphragm) to the opposite knee establishes control of the lunar plexus and sets you up for your saddle. The knee ride is a dynamic one, and being able to add the Cossack (see below) to your ride allows you much greater versatility in your ground game. Basically, whichever direction you have a free leg in when in knee-on-diaphragm determines which direction you're set to attack. If your knee closer to his hips is in his belly, then you're set for top-half game; if your knee closer to his chest is in his belly, you're set for lower-half game.

I call this the Cossack because it's exactly like a Cossack dance move we were taught in Russia. It begins with moving from the control

Top-knee ride.

Bottom-knee ride.

of riding him on the upper-half game to placing the opposite knee down on his diaphragm. When you're riding him on lower-half knee-on-diaphragm, you don't have as much control to monitor his arms from sweeps, so if you knee-switch, focus on entering the saddle without delay.

When you knee-switch, grab his near knee before you remove your knee from his diaphragm. Your other hand should control his near shoulder or wrist.

In one motion, push his shoulder down and his knee away. As soon as you do, pull your controlling knee out and immediately insert your opposite knee for lower-half game control. That's the Cossack knee switch.

At this point you'll be in the knee pinch with knee-on-diaphragm. This is a common transitional position, so don't freak out. Take a breath. I strongly suggest you drill resistance to maintain this transitional position, and get used to riding your opponent's attempts to shrimp out and away from your knee pinch. The basic escape for knee-on-diaphragm that jiujitsu fighters use is to place hands on your contacting knee and scoot the hips to the side. However, when he does this, he exposes his top knee to enter the saddle.

As his hips move away, you could Cossack knee-switch back to the top knee ride on diaphragm.

Instead of re-inserting your knee on his diaphragm, you can enter the saddle from the resistance of his knee push, and shrimp out. As you can see below, you can either enter the full or the side saddle due to this knee push.

If he pushes the inside of your knee upward, step over his downed leg to block his knee. Typically, he would never expect you to move toward his guard, so he rarely fights this setup unless he has a very developed lower-half game.

Step farther underneath his far knee and scoop it high into your lap. Keep your weight on his diaphragm with your top knee.

Grab your own ankle with your far arm, getting ready to lock it into full saddle.

As you pin his leg down with your body, pull your shin into his hip fold for the first half of the leg triangle.

Lace in your leg triangle, fire-pole down to his hip deeply, and apply the tourniquet. That will set you up for whatever happens. In this case, I demonstrate a signature combination lock of mine: a knee bar heel hook that I call a "long, slow screw."

1a and b. Bottom shrimps with knee push.

2. Cossack switch back to top knee ride.

3. Scoop top knee, step over bottom, and block downed leg.

4. Scoop knee high and step under picked knee.

5. Grab ankle with far arm.

a

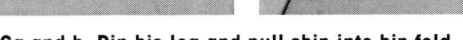

b

6a and b. Pin his leg and pull shin into hip fold.

7. Finish with a long, slow screw.

Cossack Side Saddle Variation

If you are able to step over his downed knee without him shrimping out his hips, you can also scoop his far leg in preparation for the side saddle.

Reach over with your far arm and grab your own ankle, preparing to pull your shin into his hip fold.

Pull your shin into his hip fold as you drop to your side in side saddle.

1. Drop down to side saddle; place your shin in his hip fold. Step over his near knee before he shrimps away.

2. Grab your ankle with far arm.

3. Crank into leg triangle.

4. Finish with knee bar.

1. Duck under; high crotch entry.

CROSS-MOUNT SPIN

I most often nail this off my duck-under or double-leg takedown when I switch to a high-crotch ride. When I land my opponent on the mat, I'm in top-side knee-on-diaphragm, and I still have his far knee hooked from the takedown.

2a and b. In air.

You can nail the cross-mount shin spin from knee-on-diaphragm when your opponent begins to press on your knee and scoot away.

Scoop his top knee with your near arm while pressing down on his top elbow.

With your bottom-side leg, step over or place your knee over his bottom leg to block his knee.

5. Step over bottom-side leg to block.

3. Scoop knee to bottom-side knee ride.

6. Step around and sit on elbow.

4. Scoop knee and block elbow.

7. Scoop under with opposite arm, hug thigh, and thread shin in hip fold.

8. Block near elbow or shoulder as you spin to full saddle.

With your other leg, step around the top half over his head and sit on his side, pinning his elbow to his ribs.

As soon as you sit, begin threading your shin into his hip fold, as you sit down over his back. As you do so, switch hands, scooping his top knee, and hug his thigh to your torso with your opposite arm.

If his top arm comes free, block his elbow or the shoulder of his top arm as you spin into the saddle.

Cinch up the fire pole and then lock in your leg triangle. Apply the tourniquet and let the lock appear.

9. Lock in full leg triangle.

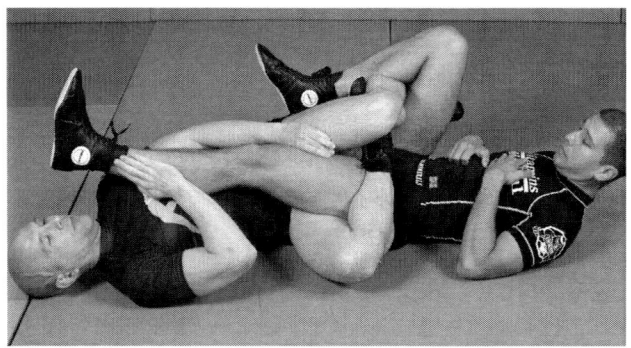

10. Fire-pole down.

11. Scoop foot behind armpit.

12. Finish with an ankle lock.

THE LAP DANCE

The lap dance happens in a double-leg takedown where you nail such a high tuck on both of his legs that, when he hits the mat, both his legs are tucked across your bottom-side thigh.

You can also enter it from the Cossack knee switch to lower-half knee-on-diaphragm with a knee pinch on the near thigh. Sometimes, your opponent will cross his legs to try to defend against the isolation.

You can also attack this proactively. If his legs are close enough, reach over with your bottom-side arm and scoop his far leg back.

Thread your arm under his opposite leg to lock in the double-ankle submission.

Although you'll get a certain percentage of your opponents right here, you won't get everyone of them just because his knee leaks leverage. He can separate his knees like a butterfly guard to lessen the effect of the lock, and pull on his own trapped ankle to drive his top ankle through to the meaty flesh of his calf.

When he does so, you can enter the saddle

2. Rotate with both legs grabbed.

1a and b. High double leg.

3. Bottom-side knee ride. Scoop far ankle high.

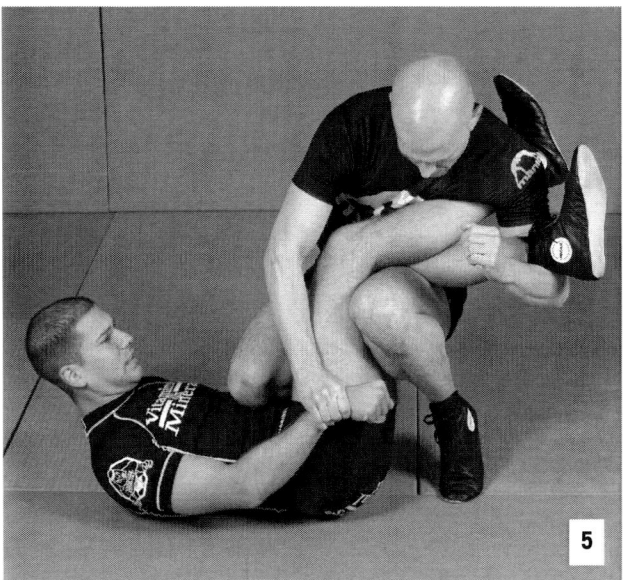

4–8. Pull high above trapped leg, and shoot arm through for double-ankle setup.

by pulling on his near thigh with your free arm. In the additional opening between his legs, weave your outside shin through to this hip fold, like the shin ride guard pass.

It's not likely that you'll be able to keep the double-ankle lock, since it limits your ability to secure the saddle position. Don't fight for it. Lock in a saddle, since position is more impor-tant than the submission. It's hard for a lot of fighters to give up on a potential lock, and they'll go down with the ship, hoping that it won't sink. It's better to throw the free-wrestling locks away and go for position first.

So, allow his legs to unlace, and twist your top leg knee down to the mat and begin crank-ing in the leg triangle. Tourniquet and finish.

9. Butterfly defense versus double leg, driving leg through.

10. Push far knee down to mat.

11. Step over with far leg.

12. Sit on his ribs; scoop double ankle.

13. Sit back and to knee pinch.

14. Finish with the double ankle.

CHAPTER 17

BASIC CROSS-SIDE SERIES

BASIC CRADLE FROM CROSS-SIDE MOUNT BLOCK

Fighters who are not familiar with the lower-half game overuse the conventional mount block from cross-side or knee-on-diaphragm. Unfortunately, for such a fighter, keeping his knee up without absolute necessity exposes it for attack. Even if your opponent only uses the block judiciously, you can fake a mount attempt to get him to expose his leg through his attempt to block.

If in cross-side, release the head and arm harness to scoop under his lifted knee with your near arm.

As you secure your hold, elbow-pit deep, roll into his diaphragm, and connect your arm, thereby trapping his leg with your arm and trapping his neck and head in the cradle, using a gable grip.

1. Mount block with knee versus cross-side head/arm harness.

2. Scoop near knee.

Now you can safely transition to knee-on-diaphragm without creating time and space for his escape. Sneak the knee for a bottom-side knee ride in without popping up. Keep it tight to your chest, and drive it up through the small opening between your locked arms and his floating ribs. Drive up until you hear his breathing become strained in the "bow" that you've created—your knee the "arrow" driving into his folded frame.

From here, overexcited fighters try to jump right into the saddle. You can sometimes pull it off, but to increase your chances for success, you should block the far hip before releasing the cradle. If he leaves his far leg straight, step over it immediately. This happens often against fighters who don't have a good lower-half game, because it can appear that he's moving you into his half-butterfly guard.

As you release the cradle, you're going to temporarily increase the pressure on his diaphragm and pull both his neck with your top-side hand and his knee with your bottom-side elbow.

Don't pull with your bottom-side hand, because you need to lever your forearm across his far thigh and drive it down to the mat. As you do, step over his far thigh with your bottom-side leg, still maintaining knee-on-diaphragm

3. Lock in the cradle. Insert the knee tightly.

4. Step over his extended leg, keep cradle.

5. Release cradle to lever down on his far thigh; increase pressure on diaphragm.

6. Step over his thigh to block far hip.

pressure. Now you can move into the saddle without the opponent being able to scoot out away from you.

If you haven't already done so, let go of his neck. Use that near-side arm to control his near shoulder or elbow. Post down on his arm as you remove your knee from his diaphragm, and insert your shin across his hip fold.

Roll toward his near shoulder. As you do, wind your shin in to bury your knee on the mat and in his ribs, before releasing his near-side elbow from your post.

Lace in your leg triangle, and secure your over-lacing foot under his sits bones. Then finalize with a lock as it appears.

Some fighters may feel this coming and attempt to bump their trapped lower leg across to your far hip. If your opponent bumps his trapped lower leg across your far hip, he sets himself up for a possible hip submission. These aren't high-percentage moves, so I don't include them in the seven core leg locks, but against inflexible fighters they work effectively. Reach up and regain the head and arm harness.

Drive your under-lacing knee backward, and kick out your over-lacing leg to drive your shin deep into his hip fold. Even if he doesn't tap out here, it allows you to roll back up into top-position cross-side.

7. Roll toward his near shoulder; wind in shin and insert knee.

8. Leg triangle, fire pole, tourniquet, and back brace.

9a–d. He bumps lower leg across.

10. Regrab harness.

11. Knee back, kick-back; smear.

PRY-BAR FROM
BOTTOM-SIDE CONTROL

A common transition for your opponent to try to pull half-guard on the bottom against your cross-side hold-down is to step over your near leg. He hopes to leg thread and scoop your leg close enough to grab it in half-guard with his other leg. You can even sometimes bait him into over-lacing your near leg by extending your leg out seemingly too far. As he responds, remove your arm from blocking his far hip, under-hook his near knee with your lower arm, and slide your leg under his thigh.

Establish this "lower cross-side" position (this is my name for it) by swinging your torso down to his lunar plexus and drive your down-side ribs into his breath. Hook his far thigh with your other arm.

Sometimes you'll be able to move into the lap dance entry from here. However, if your opponent feels that coming, he'll try to shrimp into you: put his near knee up like a mount block with his far leg extended.

1. He steps over near leg to stall or set up half-guard transition.

2. Under-hook his near knee.

3. Swing down and hook his far thigh, as you thread your leg under to bottom cross-side.

4. He shrimps into you with his near knee in and far leg extended.

Lace under his near knee and over his far thigh, and lever his far leg to the ground as you step over his far thigh to block his hip.

The mechanics to enter the saddle from here are almost identical to those for going from the basic cradle to saddle except that you must pop up to knee-on-diaphragm rather than hold the cradle and sneak in the knee.

Place your opposite forearm on the mat near his hips to prevent him from scooting out and, in one motion, pop up and slide in your knee.

5. Lace under the near thigh and over the far thigh.

6. Step over the far leg as you "leg-thread" again.

7. Post arm and pop up to bottom-side knee-on-diaphragm.

8. Scoop far leg and cross his legs.

Continue to lift his far leg until you can cross it over his near leg.

Gable-grip over the crossed leg and around the bottom, near leg. Driving down knee-on-diaphragm for the pin, lace over his over-lacing ankle with your near leg.

Roll toward his near-shoulder side. This frees your knee from his diaphragm to wrap over and cross your legs for the double-triangle, double-knee pinch.

You'll finish in the double-triangle knee bar.

9. Step over top ankle with near leg.

10a and b. Lift his far leg until you can cross it over your near leg.

11. Finish with a double triangle knee bar.

BALL AND CHAIN
(*KIMURA* SADDLE TRANSITION)

Enter the basic *kimura,* or hammer-lock, submission from cross-side top as normal: far elbow blocking hip, wrist control, slide up, under-lace near arm, wrist rotation, and step up and over to block shoulder.

To protect his arm from kimura, the opponent reaches between his legs with the attacked arm to grab his pants or inside of his thigh.

If his arm remains bent, he exposes himself to an elbow slice. However, top-half submission fighting isn't the focus, so I'll save the details of that game for another book.

If he protects his elbow from the slice by extending it out correctly, scoop up outside the top thigh and grab his wrist from underneath (in folk-style wrestling, this is called the ball and chain hold).

1. Basic *kimura* from cross-side top.

2. Cross-side elbow blocking far hip.

3. Wrist control and slide up under-lace arm.

It is critical that you sit down heavily on his side belly/diaphragm. You thus remain in position for the saddle and yet still in control of him: ball and chain and sitting on his diaphragm, blocking his hip with your inserted foot.

To saddle up, first shove your leg through, pointing your toes. At this point, you can release the ball and chain. With the same hand, grab your own foot for a temporary arm-and-leg triangle on his thigh.

4. Wrist rotation.

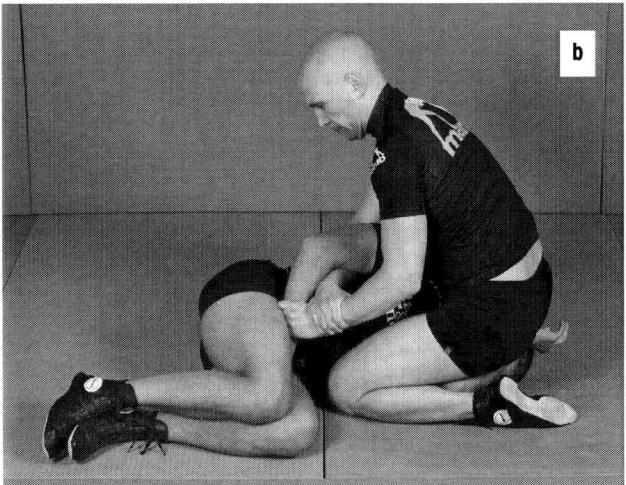

5a and b. Step up and over head to block rear shoulder.

6. Scoop in the ball and chain.

7. Push down on his head and pull up on ball and chain.

Slide your hips down to the outside (along his back). This will turn him from his side to his back.

Get your shin in his hip fold, and get your knee on the mat. On the way down, lock in the lace; if he fights, concentrate more on getting the knee down and in his ribs—the most important part for maintaining positional dominance. Once the knee is in place, bring your top-side knee under your arm, holding your foot to crank in the leg triangle.

Once the knee's in, lace your legs together for the full leg triangle, and bury your unprotected foot between his sits bones. Then just wait for him to give you the sub of his choice.

8. Step over his head and around and over his bottom leg.

9. Sit down on his floating ribs, with his arm still trapped.

10. Shove leg in, point toes, release ball and chain, and grab your own foot.

11. Knee down; crank to leg triangle.

12. Fire-pole, tourniquet, and hit the "GQ" knee bar.

1. Bottom cross-side control versus opponent scooting to side.

BANANA SPLIT FROM BOTTOM-SIDE CROSS TOP

From bottom cross-side top, an opponent often tries to scoot out toward half-guard.

A common jiujitsu counter is to step over your near, under-side leg with his top leg to try to climb to half-guard top. Gladly accept this, and bury it as deeply as possible with your knee into his crotch and your calf on his hamstring. You've locked in half of the reverse saddle already, thanks to him.

Reach over and grab his opposite ankle, pulling it toward his buttocks. This will secure both of his hips and, as a result, his lunar plexus for the roll.

Perform a lateral shoulder (Granby) roll while scooping, holding his ankle. This roll is difficult if you haven't practiced it. (I strongly suggest Prasara body-flow yoga daily for submission fighters. Roll first to your back.)

2. He steps over you; bury his leg.

4a and b. Lateral shoulder roll to your back.

While rolling, lock in the leg triangle for the reverse-saddle position.

From here, you have several options. I'll give you a few examples of higher-percentage moves for those proficient at lower-half position fighting.

If you adjust your knee outward until the bottom third of your shin is behind his knee, you can finalize with a knee slice. Reach up and pull his ankle downward, while kicking your over-lacing leg straight, to press your shin deeper into his knee pit. This will separate his knee and cause excruciating pain.

If, however, you maintain his ankle and continue to drive your under-laced leg into the inside of his thigh, you can regrip under his entire opposite thigh to enter the banana split. Drive your leg triangle away as you hug his thigh to your chest. You want to outwardly rotate both legs as you separate them like a turkey wishbone. Most inflexible fighters will tap early just from causing the straddle split to the groin. However, to ensure the highest percentage of success, focus on outwardly rotating both thighs simultaneously. This minimizes his potential range of motion and causes extreme discomfort.

If your opponent is very flexible, you can release this top thigh and kick your leg triangle down to the mat. Maintain control of his outside thigh by weaving your far arm over to his waist. You've now entered the rear-saddle position.

Typically, fighters want to avoid going to their belly with you in back position. To prevent you from getting into a full back position, an opponent will often turn toward you, exposing his top arm. Grab it and lift it over your head behind your neck. Make sure to clear your near-side arm high, and reach over his head.

5. Adjust knee out, sink to bottom one-third, pull ankle, and straighten leg.

6. Reach under and hug thigh for banana split.

7. Kick over to back position rear saddle.

8. Grab his top arm and move behind your head while clearing your near arm behind his.

Gable-grip your hands together. Simultaneously drive your rear saddle underneath while turning his head and arm in the opposite direction on top. In folk-style wrestling, this is called a twister, though it has been popularized in submission fighting by Eddie Bravo.

If your opponent releases his arm, or if he turns to his belly, maintain the rear saddle and finalize with an arm triangle choke.

These types of attacks are not the central focus of this book; however, it's important to reiterate that the greater the credibility of your threats upstairs, the stronger the effectiveness of your attacks downstairs!

9a and b. Finalize the twister.

10a–d. Rear-saddle, back-position arm triangle choke.

CHAPTER 18

SEATED GUARD SERIES

BASIC ANKLE PICK

The basic ankle pick is a common variation on the shin swing, which begins with a butt scoot toward the opponent, while seated.

I find it most effective to scoop my own foot behind his ankle and pull at the same time that I pull the ankle with my near arm.

1. Butt scoot versus shin squat.

2. Insert knee and pick ankle.

Most often, jiujitsu fighters will try to step with it in hopes of passing your guard, at least to the half-guard position. But that sets you up for inserting your knee behind his leg.

If he's flat-footed on the floor, heist your hips up toward his and drive your shoulders into the ground to get your shin over his thigh and to his hip fold. Make sure to block his far knee with your shin.

3. He steps to half guard. Bury knee and block the far knee with shin.

4a and b. Hip-heist shoulder bridge and insert shin into hip fold; block the far knee with shin.

5a and b. Grab his foot for temporary triangle.

Once he hits the ground, pass your shin over the top and bury your knee on the mat. If he falls fast, you may need to temporarily grab your own foot with your far arm. Try to do this by reaching under your other leg if you can.

Crank your foot into a leg triangle before he hits the ground.

Scoop up his attacked knee with your hands, and fire pole down to bury the shin in his hip fold as tightly as possible.

Fight your knee into the mat and in his ribs. Then back-brace to set up the finishing hold.

6. Crank in leg triangle.

7. Scoop and fire-pole.

8. Finish with an Achilles submission.

DIRTBALL SWEEP

After you've picked an ankle from seated guard and inserted your shin in his hip fold, if your opponent remains standing, he may lean into you, chest to chest. He'll be in half-mount, with your leg over his thigh. To sweep him from there, move just as if you were whipping around to half-guard, but with a few differences.

Get under-hooks with a gable grip if possible. If not, under-hook his elbows and then lift him overhead. Use your shin in his hip fold to roll yourself into a ball, by contracting your leg toward your chest.

As he posts both arms down to prevent his going too far overhead, take your arm on the side of your attacking leg and reach under his chest to his opposite shoulder, blocking it with your forearm.

1. Half-leg triangle ankle pick versus standing but bending over.

2a–d. Double under-hooks. Lift to make him post.

To spin on your back like this, you must adjust your shin from his hip fold to the inside of his thigh.

If you can, lock down your leg triangle from here. Even if you cannot, the sweep will work.

3. Block far shoulder and spin perpendicular.

4a and b. Sweep him toward his trapped leg.

Place your other hand at his hip. With your arm braced in his armpit, simultaneously push up and drive your shin into the inside of his trapped thigh. Push in the direction of the leg you have trapped, which is at a diagonal from his base.

Sometimes, to finish this, you'll have to remove the forearm pushing on his armpit and quickly scoop his attacked ankle again to return to the ankle pick described above.

5a–c. Knee to mat; scoop knee, fire-pole, tourniquet, and back brace.

BUTTERFLY ANKLE PICK

Sometimes your opponent will have a strong stance and defend against your over-hooking leg. He'll try to take your shin out of his hip fold.

Since he exposes his hand when he pops off your ankle, get wrist control with your near arm, even if he clears your foot to his ribs.

With your other hand, pick his far ankle and place your far shin on the inside of his knee, as if in a half-butterfly guard.

1. Ankle pick versus standing clearing shin.

2. Scoop far ankle and insert shin to far leg.

Simultaneously drive your wrist control back in the direction of his butt and down toward the mat, while picking his far ankle and driving your shin over his knee. To understand the sweep on his far leg, think of pulling his heel inward with your hand, as you rotate your knee over his knee while pushing with your shin. You want to cause the outside of his knee to collapse down toward the mat. Lift your hips off the mat to get sufficient heist.

You'll have his primary ankle under your armpit when you hit the mat together. In your other hand will be his far ankle. Pull on both to fire-pole up the back of his thigh. You'll be in knee-pinch position.

As you do this, place your foot on the inside of his far knee and release his far ankle as you drive away with your foot, straddling him.

Reach up and grab your attacking-leg foot and pull your shin into his hip fold. If possible, at the same time, adjust your knee to the mat, preparing for him to pull into you. This may require that you rotate your far leg into his knee pit as if you were performing a side kick: foot sword in knee-pit, with heel rotating up and toes down.

3. Pull down on wrist, push out on knee, and rotate in on ankle; hip heist.

4. Pull on both of his legs to fire-pole close into knee pinch.

5. Straddle-drive his far leg away.

6. Grab your own foot with far arm and pull shin into hip fold, knee to mat; rotate your kick-away leg.

Release his far leg with your foot. Release your own ankle from your grip. Insert the leg triangle to establish full saddle.

Scoop the knee and fire-pole down to apply the tourniquet. Lock in your back brace and prepare the setup to finish him. In this case, I demonstrate the "Fantastic Four" heel hook—a signature move I created to prevent slippery feet from escaping. You'll love this one.

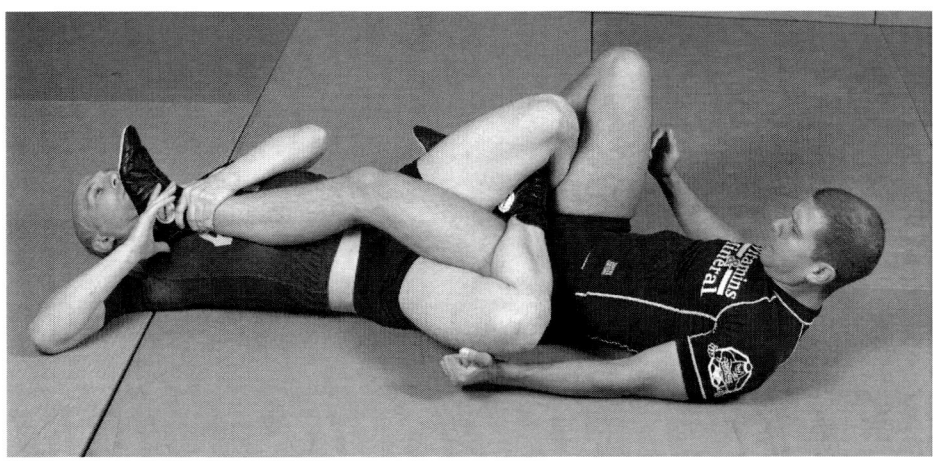

7. Release his leg and your ankle to leg triangle.

8a–c. Scoop, fire-pole, tourniquet, and back brace. Finish with the Fantastic Four heel hook.

THE PICK SWITCH

Your opponent is still standing after you pick his ankle and insert your thigh into his hip fold. As he steps backward with his opposite leg to keep his base, place your far foot in his far hip fold (like spider guard).

Switch your near-leg foot into his armpit. If his arm is down fighting to unlace your leg, then get wrist control. As you allow him to release your lace, place your foot in his armpit.

In one motion, drive his wrist down to the side of your body while switching your legs. Your far leg shoots from his far hip, deep into his near hip fold.

Move your foot from his near shoulder to

1. Standing with leg back versus ankle pick.

2. Place your far foot in his far hip fold.

3a and b. Place near leg in near armpit; wrist control.

slam your top knee down into leg triangle side saddle, to cause the takedown. Rotate this thigh externally by pushing your under-lacing knee high with a hip heist shoulder bridge, and drive your over-lacing foot down toward the ground.

As he falls, bend your over-lacing leg foot toward your buttocks and get it as high as possi-ble so that his weight doesn't land on it. If you can, reach underneath and rustle it back under his buttocks.

Now on the ground, he tries to roll to his back to sit up. Rotate the under-laced knee down to lock in the side saddle. Finish with an internal heel hook.

4. Switch off far hip to across near inside thigh and drive wrist down.

5. Lock in leg triangle side saddle to externally rotate his attacked leg.

6. Rustle over-lacing leg.

7. Fight the inside knee down to side saddle, fire-pole, tourniquet, and back brace. Finish with internal heel hook.

THE SCISSORS-GUARD ENTRY

With your opponent in your scissors half-guard, and your top shin on his belly, control his wrists. When he forces forward, hoping to pass your top knee, he'll post his far leg out flat-footed.

Under-hook his far thigh with your near arm, and lock his near armpit with your opposite forearm.

Draw your knee from between his legs up behind his thigh as you begin a spinal roll backward toward your head.

Your outside leg will cross over his hamstring, beginning the reverse saddle. Lace in the triangle and tuck your over-lacing leg between his sits bones.

Fire-pole up, apply the tourniquet, and finalize with a "draw-bridge" knee bar.

1. Scissors half-guard.

2. Posts flat foot.

3. Under-hook thigh; block near armpit.

4. Roll back and insert underside leg behind his far thigh.

6a–c. Fire-pole, tourniquet. Finish with knee-bar behind arm and block far leg to prevent rolling.

5a–c. Lace in leg triangle for reverse saddle.

SCISSORS-GUARD RECOUNTER

Be careful with the scissors half-guard, because your opponent can recounter your saddle entry with one of his own (which I, like some coaches, call a recounter).

In your opponent's scissors guard, over-hook and scoop his top knee with your near arm.

Drive off your back leg into his shin, and lift on his knee across your centerline. Drive your shoulder down to the mat at your opponent's back. This will roll him to his back as you lace your shin into his hip fold.

1. Saddle entry versus scissors.

3a and b. Lift his knee across centerline and drive off back leg.

Scoop his knee and fire-pole down to get your knee to the mat. Follow with a leg triangle and back brace to set up the final hold.

4. Shoulder to mat, lace-in shin to hip fold.

5a–c. Leg triangle, fire-pole, and fight knee to mat; back brace.

REVERSE-SADDLE KNEE SWIRLY

As you enter into the reverse saddle, your opponent may scramble to clear his knee between your legs, or you may have failed to fire-pole high enough to secure his leg.

When this happens, reach with your near arm and under-hook his near hip. If you can't do this, you can grab his wrist to pull up, but this move is more difficult to time.

Slide your knee to the inside to insert the bottom one-third of your shin as deeply into the back of his knee as possible.

Here you can secure the conventional sambo knee-slice, bringing his heel to his tailbone. However, for opponents with thick legs, this can be difficult, especially if you have thick calves.

If, however, you drive the hip of your leg behind his knee toward his, you will cause this hip to externally rotate. This knee "swirly" causes a faster and more painful submission, due to the spiral separation of the hip and the lateral shear on the knee, in addition to the standard knee-leveraged slice.

Lock in your leg triangle and drive your over-lacing leg into your under-lacing knee in order to penetrate your shin into his knee pit as deeply as possible.

1a and b. Shallow reverse saddle.

2. Slide knee out to bottom one-third of shin into the back of his knee.

3. Move knee around from near hamstring to far hamstring.

CHAPTER 19

X-GUARD SERIES

FIGURE-8 X-GUARD SWEEP TO SADDLE

This sweep is a very, very cool transition to move in and out of saddle, X-guard, and side saddle. I named it "Figure-8" because it's almost the exact same motion as an ice-climbing maneuver, where you have to weave your shins inside your own arms to get leverage to lift yourself.

If you face a standing opponent with a strong but narrow base and you have the ankle pick set up, he often tries to pop off your ankle from his hip. As he tries to pop your ankle, move from the ankle pick in order to scoop and under-hook his calf to your shoulder.

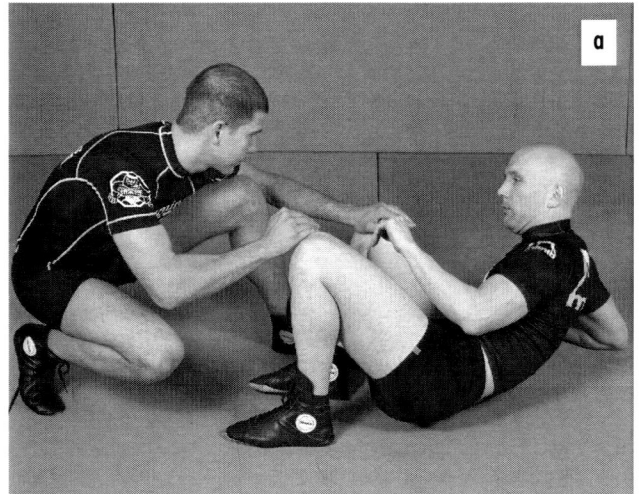

1a and b. Standing versus ankle pick.

Move from this inverted knee pinch to extend your far knee outward like the butterfly ankle pick entry.

Allow him to pop off your foot and use that energy to weave that shin under his far thigh for X-guard.

As soon as you have the second shin in to complete the X-guard, press off that second shin, and weave your front shin over his opposite leg (the leg you initially attacked).

Kick your other leg knee toward your chest and lock in the leg triangle side saddle.

If you have flexibility issues, I've found some fighters need to use a crank to get their foot in place, or to hold the leg triangle until sweeping the opponent to the mat. Since you already have under-hooked his leg, your hand is free to crank in the triangle.

To finish the sweep, pivot on your shoulder blades to screw his attacked thigh over, externally rotating his knee.

As he goes down and his weight is freed from his foot, reach over and hook it under your armpit in the back brace.

Rotate your inside knee down between his sits bones. Rustle your far ankle in, if you have to protect it. Tourniquet and finish with an ankle lock.

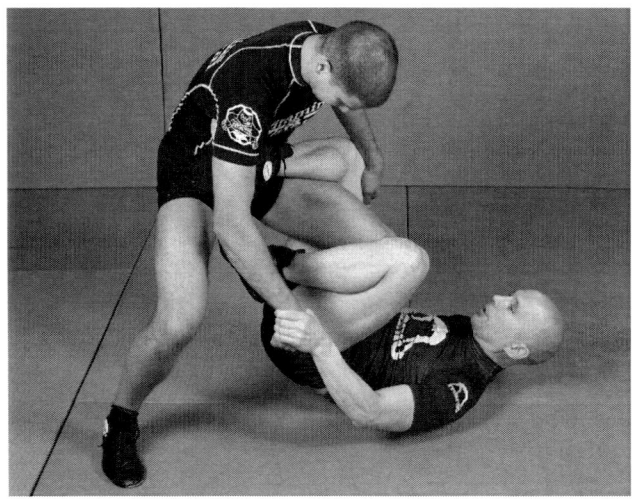

2. He pops off ankle. Scoop under his attacked ankle and knee pinch.

3. Insert half butterfly on far leg.

4a and b. Weave top leg between his legs for X-guard.

5. Press off top leg to weave bottom over near thigh.

6. Kick back knee toward your chest to lace triangle side saddle.

7. Crank in triangle.

8. Pivot on shoulder blades.

9. Insert back brace.

10. Rustle in far leg, fire-pole, tourniquet, and finish with an ankle lock.

BULLFROG BUTTERFLY TO REVERSE FIGURE-8

The bullfrog is an adaptation of a jiujitsu setup to X-guard, and an easy variation once you've mastered the figure-8. The figure-8 is the basis of all transitions between the saddles and the X-guards, so master it first.

Start sitting, facing each other, and keep your feet together and scoot in to butterfly. Get double under-hooks and a gable grip. Spinal roll back and elevate your shins.

When he goes to his feet, insert your leg behind him to foot-hook his opposite thigh, while simultaneously under-hooking the opposite leg with your arm to lock in the X-guard.

1. Seated versus seated scoot to double butterfly.

2. Double under-hooks gable grip.

3. Spinal-roll and elevate your shins.

4. Foot-hook far thigh and under-hook near calf.

If you've been practicing, your opponent may be expecting the standard figure-8 now. The following variation is the exact opposite of the figure-8 and will surprise your opponent, especially if he starts defending the normal figure-8 too early to recognize the reverse figure-8. As soon as he stands to try to pass, push off the bottom of the X with your legs and roll back with the top of your X to land your shin in his hip fold.

Chase the bottom of your X, knee to chest. Reach under your knee to grab your own foot if you can't lock in the leg triangle immediately.

Under-hook your over-lacing foot under his sits bones, if he has a shallow stance; or under his far thigh, if he has a narrow stance.

Reach up and grab near-arm wrist control when he tries to break your leg triangle. Drive his wrist down. Execute a hip-heist shoulder bridge high and drive his knee outward, exter-

5. Insert top shin of X-guard over his hip fold.

6. Put your knee to his chest to crank in leg triangle. Under-hook with over-lacing leg.

7. Wrist-control his near arm; externally rotate knee with hip heist to sweep.

nally rotating it to sweep him.

Fire-pole with a knee scoop, bury the knee into his ribs and on the mat, and apply the tourniquet. Bump his lower leg across, apply the back brace, and finish him with the Fantastic Four heel hook.

8a–d. Fire-pole, knee down, tourniquet, bump across, back brace, and finish with the **Fantastic Four.**

1. X-guard grab near wrist control.

DOGTAIL X-GUARD SWEEP

From X-guard, grab your opponent's near wrist if possible.

Drive your X into the inside of his trapped thigh. Simultaneously, pull his opposite knee down toward your chest, while keeping his opposite foot trapped by your shoulder. Pull his wrist out away from your body, as if to sprawl his body parallel to the mat.

At the last moment before he can post, yank his hand inward toward your hips, and you will cause him to perform a shoulder roll. You can prevent his roll here instead, and allow him to post both arms out. Lace in your reverse saddle leg triangle.

2. Drive X away, pull knee inward, extend wrist, and elevate X.

3. Yank wrist to cause shoulder roll.

4. Lace in leg triangle for reverse saddle.

5. Surf to knee-pin guard pass.

I suggest practicing the full version. Most fighters will try to pull guard, which means that they will try to roll under to their backs, so you need to know how to surf all the way through.

Surf his roll all the way to his back. You must pin down his opposite thigh with the shin on the bottom of your X (knee toward his belly) to avoid him pulling guard.

With his knee on your shoulder, drive your shoulder toward his far shoulder, while maintaining a lock on the inside of his opposite thigh with your shin. This may submit inflexible fighters.

If it does not result in submission, you can transition into a reverse saddle knee-bar.

6. Extend groin toward far shoulder.

7. Clear his far leg and lock in the triangle with your top leg rustled under his ribs.

8. Fire-pole down deeply.

9. Hold his ankle with your bottom arm as you weave your top arm under his leg.

10. Post down and apply the knee bar pressure in a corkscrew.

1. X-guard grab near wrist control.

SHINBOX X-GUARD SWEEP

From X-guard, grab your opponent's near wrist if possible.

Split your X-guard so that the bottom foot hooks his ankle and top-hooks his knee. Pull on his ankle and push on his knee with your split X-guard.

Simultaneously, gable-grip your hands around the outside of his knee. By pulling, rotate his knee down toward your same-side hip, while keeping his opposite foot trapped by your shoulder.

2. Split the X and push/pull.

3. Gable-grip and pull.

4. With knee down, high-step over the trapped leg.

As he goes down to his butt, your rear knee will touch the mat first. As soon as it does, high-step over his trapped leg.

Weave your high-stepping leg under his hamstring. Continue rotating over to get your knee under his leg, between his crotch. Immediately scoop his knee and fire-pole down.

Lace in the side-saddle leg triangle, tourniquet, and back-brace to finish.

5. Weave high-stepping leg under.

6a and b. Rotate to side saddle prep, scoop knee, fire-pole down, and back-brace.

7. Lock in Achilles and rustle in over-lacing leg.

1a and b. X-guard, passes front knee down.

2. Roll back and insert rear shin to hip fold.

TOILET SEAT X-GUARD
SWEEP TO SADDLE

If you are in the X-guard, he tries to step out to get away by passing your front knee down and then transitioning to a variation of the ankle pick or pick switch.

Roll toward your shoulders and lace your rear leg over his trapped leg. Slide your shin in as deep into his hip fold as the position permits.

As your opponent steadies himself to balance the attacked leg, he'll remove his hands from the knee he passed. Drive that bottom foot into the inside of his far knee.

Like the opposite direction of a shinbox sweep, with your near hand, pull the inside of his top knee to rotate it outward in a circle.

As he falls, grab your near foot and slide it fully into his hip fold, since your knee will be in place on the mat when he hits.

3. As he falls, grab your foot for temporary triangle.

Drive the far knee away, keeping a hold on your temporary arm and leg triangle. As he's falling, lock in your leg triangle.

Rustle in your top leg, fire-pole down, slam on the tourniquet, and go for the finish.

4. Drive far knee away.

5. Rustle in your over-lacing leg to his sits bones.

6. Reach under and over his trapped leg.

7a and b. Finish with an internal heel hook.

CHAPTER 20

TURTLE SERIES

SUICIDE CRADLE TO SADDLE

The suicide cradle starts when you're in top position with your opponent in turtle.

Reach under his near-side neck and scoop up his far elbow, while faking an ankle pick on his near side. It doesn't need to be a fake. You can roll him from here into the basic cradle.

However, if he steps out with his far leg to keep base, he creates a knee-to-head relationship perfect for the cradle. Release his ankle and his elbow, and scoop between his bracing knee and his near-side neck to secure the cradle in a gable grip.

At the same time, dive over your cradle

1. Cross-side versus turtle.

2. Wrap neck and elbow; pick ankle.

3. He steps out to base; you lock cradle.

along the back of his far arm to roll him to his back. Screw your arms while rolling, lifting with the arm under his thigh and driving underneath with the arm under his neck and across his chest.

You land in position to execute the basic cradle-to-saddle entry.

4a and b. Dive forward to roll.

5. Cross-side top cradle.

6. Insert knee for bottom-side knee ride; step over bottom leg.

7. Release cradle; block shoulder.

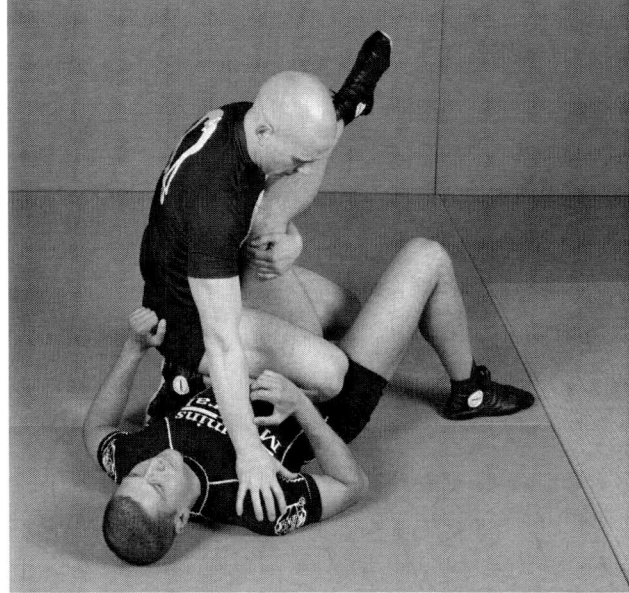

8. Step shin into hip fold.

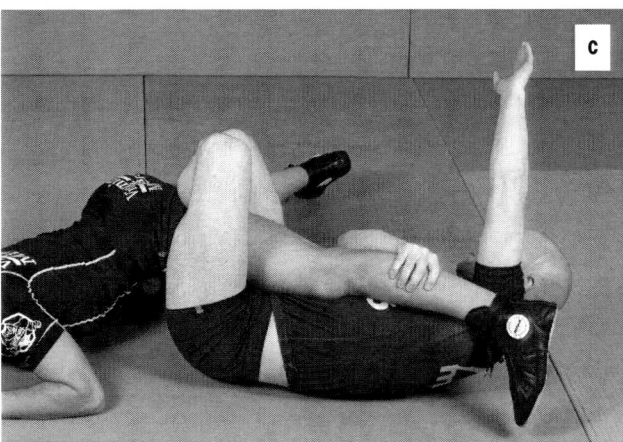

9a–d. Knee to mat, leg triangle, rustle, fire pole, tourniquet, and back brace. Finish with a knee bar.

BANANA SPLIT TO REAR SADDLE

This variation starts with you attempting to lock down the cradle on his turtle position just like in the suicide cradle, but he counters by widening his base with his legs and extending his near knee toward you.

In one motion, you release his head and lace your near leg into the hip fold of his near leg. If you break his base and he goes to his belly, you may be able to go into a twister variation. If, however, he begins to roll to his back when you're in rear-saddle turtle, you gable-grip his far thigh with both arms and simultaneously lock in the leg triangle on his trapped leg.

You land in the banana split. Most inflexible fighters will tap early, just from causing the straddle split to the groin. However, to ensure the highest percentage of success, focus on outwardly rotating both thighs simultaneously. This minimizes his potential range of motion and causes extreme discomfort.

Remember the positional flow suggested earlier:

- Kick over to back-position rear saddle.
- Grab top arm and move behind your head, while clearing your near arm behind his.
- Finalize the twister.
- Continue to the rear-saddle back-position arm triangle choke.

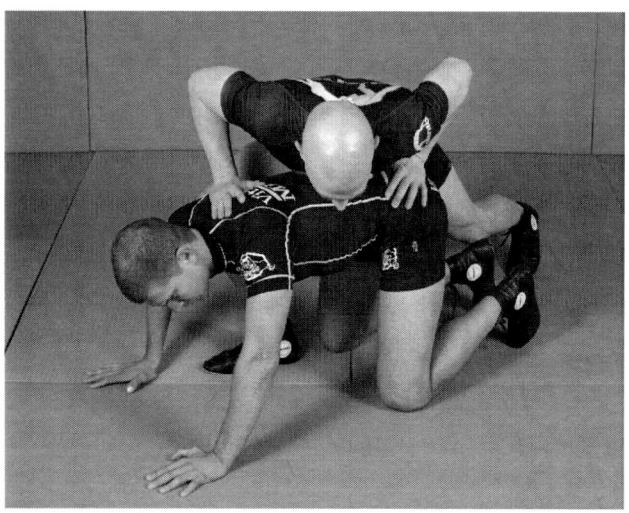

1. Cradle attempt versus wide-base turtle.

2. Insert your near leg into his hip fold for half rear saddle.

3a and b. As he rolls, you hug his far thigh. Leg triangle trapped thigh.

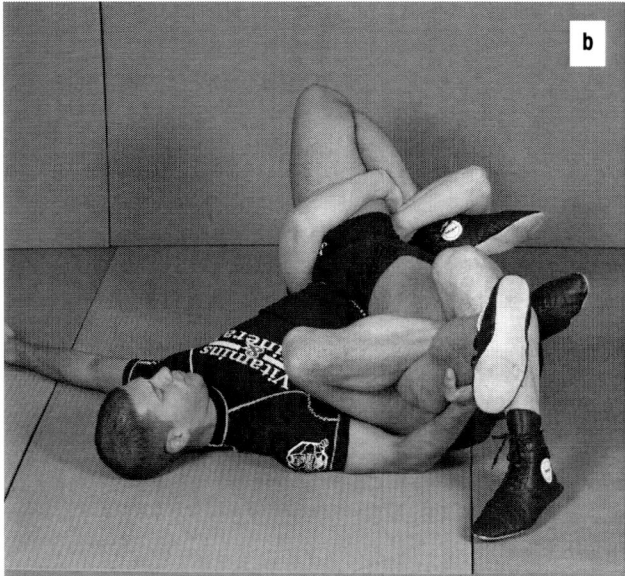

4a–c. Reach under and hug thigh for banana split.

TURTLE SEAT-BELT ROLL TO SADDLE

Perform this entry just like you would a standing seat belt roll described in the next section. Begin in cross-side top, with your opponent in turtle. Make sure you load your hip down to prevent him from sitting out.

Keep a firm seat-belt hold, and run a half

nelson under his near arm, attempting to turn him over to cross-side.

Bring your far hip to his near side to release hip pressure. This baits him into stepping up his near knee. Stronger fighters will try to power-out by doing this, without you even releasing hip pressure.

Insert your near leg between his, and slide

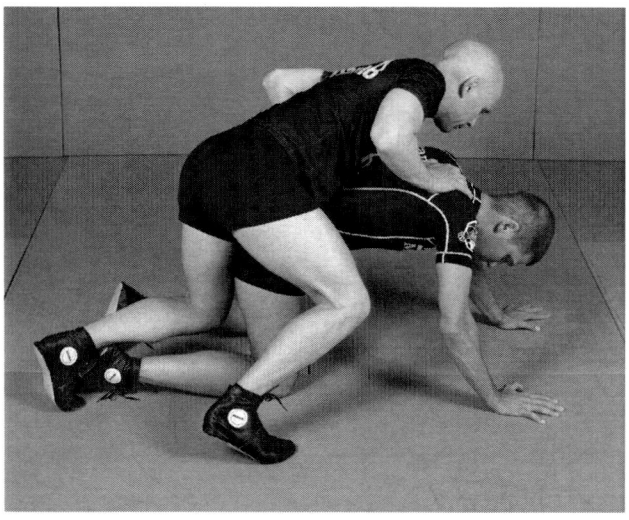

1. Cross-side top versus turtle.

2. Run near half nelson.

3. Do a seat belt around his back with your other arm.

4. Step through to near side; he brings knee up to sit up.

your arm out of the half nelson and down to scoop the outside of his knee.

Reap your inside leg high between his crotch. Get your chest all the way flush with his thigh, while pulling on your seat belt. Grab up toward your far shoulder. Drive off your planted foot away diagonally to roll.

Hold the seat belt and thigh hug tight as you roll in a half reverse saddle. Lace in the leg triangle while rolling to complete the reverse saddle.

5. Insert your near leg and scoop knee; keep the seat belt.

6a–c. Reap high, chest to thigh, seatbelt pull, foot drive. Lace in leg triangle while rolling for reverse saddle.

Scoot up the fire pole and apply the tourniquet. If his trapped leg crosses top, swim your arm in for the knee bar.

If his trapped leg crosses bottom, insert your arm, step over, and do a knee slice, as discussed earlier.

7a–c. Rustle in top lace, fire-pole, tourniquet, and swim arm to knee bar.

1. Bottom-side turtle wrist control defense.

ROLLING SADDLE FROM BOTTOM TURTLE

As your opponent takes back position with you in turtle, defend your neck by feinting wrist control.

If he has a poor back mount ride, he'll be too high, and you can shoulder-throw him over to his back. If he has a good back mount ride, he'll be

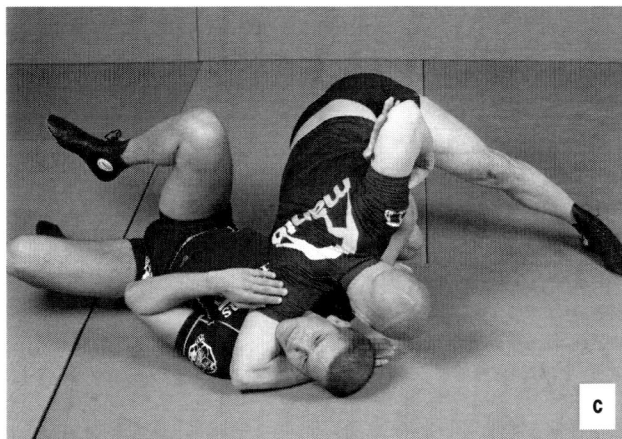

2a–d. Shoulder throw to scarf (head/arm hold-down).

low on your hips. If he is low on your hips, place your head on the mat and lift your hips. Wait for one of his legs to move between your legs, or step out with one leg as a base. (Just be careful that you don't create a knee-head relationship, for him to nail the suicide cradle on you.) When one of his legs is between your own, tuck your head under and scoop his calf with your far arm.

3. Lift hips on low hip ride.

4a and b. Scoop ankle between your legs; tuck head.

Heist his crotch with your inside leg between his as you roll him over.

Get your knee down, lock in the triangle, fire-pole, tourniquet, and finish.

5a and b. Elevate inside reap.

6a and b. Leg triangle, knee down, fire-pole, tourniquet, back brace, and finish.

STANDING SADDLE ENTRIES

Once you have trained to incorporate the saddle in your ground-fighting game, you can begin to practice getting into the saddle as a takedown and throw. This is very difficult for people, especially when they are in the mind-set that they're jumping for a leg lock—the old fast-wrestling mentality. These takedowns require practice.

However, once you've developed them, you multiply your stand-up tactics, expand your technical abilities, and, frankly, scare the crap out of most fighters who don't even like you looking at their legs, much less separating their sinews in the most torturous ways imaginable.

ROLLING SADDLE

A basic entry, the rolling saddle is a variation that I originally had to implement against fighters with a strong base. Please don't confuse a rolling saddle with a rolling knee bar, often called "Viktor's roll" in sambo. Named after the man who invented it in competition, Viktor's roll is very effective in sport sambo, but it's a technique erupting from a fast-wrestling approach and can be difficult to apply against 80 percent of the MMA fighters out there, who will know how to exploit the "slop" that you've created by jumping for the leg, like a dog in heat.

The primary differences between the saddle roll and Viktor's roll are as follows:

- In the saddle, you land with your opponent's knee bent; in Viktor's roll, you land in the knee bar straight. This is important, because if Viktor's roll fails, you need to know how to deal with the opponent defending his legs. His first defense is crossing his feet.
- In the saddle roll, you screw around your opponent's leg with your head and shoulder actually breaking the plane between his knees while he's standing. In Viktor's roll, you marry his chest to your opponent's shin, and land with the knee bar on before hitting the ground. Viktor's roll is more of a free-wrestling

approach, whereas the rolling saddle is predominantly for establishing and maintaining positional dominance.

- The saddle roll is learned and practiced no-gi/jacketless by grabbing across to the bottom of your opponent's lats/floating ribs. In Viktor's roll, you grab the belt of the sambo *kurtka* and pull your opponent over as you hit the knee bar. You can't do that without a jacket, so the seat belt attaches to his far waist, which is why you roll at a 45-degree angle in the seat belt; as opposed to in Viktor's roll, during which he roll goes directly forward, back to the belly.

You apply the rolling saddle by rolling diagonally from the back of one shoulder across to the opposite hip. As you go to the ground, secure your opponent's knee with your near hand so that you can fire-pole up toward his hip while you're rolling.

You can move in from practically any clinch, but, optimally, I prefer to move in the same slow, methodical fashion in my clinch game that I do on the ground: wrist control to two-on-one tie, to under-hook or hip control. Once you attach to the hip, getting into the saddle is rather simple. When you get really good at it, you can nail it pretty easily from virtually anywhere once you've established a good clinch.

The following photos illustrate a saddle roll into a near knee bar.

1. Two-on-one clinch.

2. Fake far-foot sweep.

3. Move to seat belt on waist, with wrist control.

4. Inside reap; hip high to saddle; hook trapped knee with outside arm; pull belly to his thigh.

5. Pull seat belt to screw between his legs; drive wrist control through legs; hold on through roll.

6. With him on his back, you fight your knee back down to the mat.

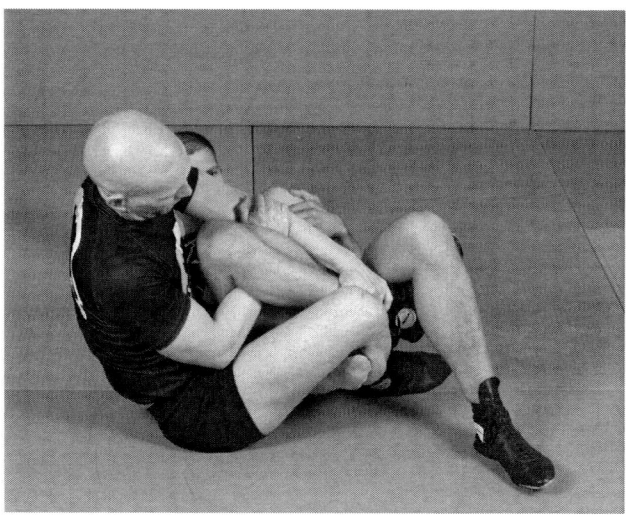

7. Lace leg triangle.

8a and b. Finish with knee bar swim or knee slice.

There are four other rolling leg attacks, which I illustrate below but do not discuss in this book (these are topics for another book):

1. Scissors cut-back throw—*kanibasame.*

2. Leg lace (lead-leg hook)—my competition favorite!
3. Leg lace screw—my signature takedown, which I have nailed many times for wins.
4. Leg lace lift—*kawazugake.*

1. Scissors cut-back throw.

3. Leg lace screw.

2. Leg lace (lead-leg hook).

4. Leg lace lift.

CHAPTER 22

CONCLUSION? NEVER

I wish I could say with absolute confidence that what you have read here will always be true, but that flies in the face of reality. The saddle is only one fraction of the total groundfighting game, which doesn't include stand-up grappling, striking and kicking, and all of the subsystems within them.

In today's world of mixed martial arts, we rush to embrace the notion that we've found the ultimate elixir of fighting technique, tactics, and strategies. But with each century that passes, every martial art changes as dramatically as the rest of civilization. Just look at how much has changed in the past 30 years!

As jiujitsu was in the 1990s, sambo will likely be the next sensation in martial arts because of its success at the highest levels of mixed martial arts competition. Sambo's forefathers set the stage for this success almost exactly 100 years ago with their willingness to investigate, study, experiment, and implement anything they found useful for increasing combat efficiency and effectiveness.

This book intends to carry on the spirit of that open-minded, inclusive, ever-evolving mission. With the publishing of this book, I know that I will have refined my material more, with each new fighter who trains, adapts, and evolves . . . and returns to our sweat-, tear-, and blood-encrusted laboratory of a gym.

Sambo practitioners will continue to practice and compete, to pressure-test results in the cauldron of actual competition, so years from that now I'm sure we'll have expanded our game, changed some approaches, and scrapped a lot of ideas. Amidst this constant evolution, however, some universal mechanics remain constant, and those are what you have studied those in this book. Remember, however, it is how you implement what you have learned that will determine whether they will work for you.

Keep the evolution going.

GLOSSARY

A-B-C-D

Achilles lock, or hold—a submission hold that causes pain from application of force to the Achilles tendon.

abduction—movement toward the centerline of the body.

adduction—movement away from the centerline of the body.

aikido—a Japanese martial art developed by Morihei Ueshiba translated as the way of unifying (with) life energy. Ueshiba's goal was to create an art that practitioners could use to defend themselves while also protecting their attacker from injury by blending with the motion of the attacker and redirecting the force of the attack rather than opposing it head-on. One leads the opponent's momentum using entering and turning movements. The techniques are completed with various throws or joint locks.

aikijutsu—a form of jujutsu that emphasizes early neutralization of an attack. Like other forms of jujutsu, it emphasizes throwing techniques and joint manipulations to effectively control, subdue or injure an attacker. It emphasizes using the timing of an attack to either blend or neutralize its effectiveness and use the force of the attacker's movement against them. It is characterized by the ample use of *atemi*, or the striking of vital areas, in order to set up their joint-locking or throwing tactics

All-Russian Federation of Martial Arts (RFRMA) (Russian)—recognized by the Ministry of Sport and the Russian Olympic Committee as the official agency representing Russian martial arts for the Russian government.

ankle lock—a submission hold that causes pain from the hyperextension of the ankle joint.

ankle pick—a takedown, or sweep, where one pulls the ankle to unbalance the opponent.

armbar—a submission hold that causes pain from the hyperextension of the elbow joint

arm triangle—a holding method using both of one's arms, one hand in the elbow pit of the other, to create a "figure-4" lace around the opponent's body part.

Ashtanga—a system of yoga that is characterized by a focus on dynamic connecting posture, that creates a flow between the more static traditional yoga postures, linking of the movement to the breath. Unlike some yoga styles, attention is also placed on the journey between the postures not just the postures themselves.

back mount—a control position on the ground, where one holds the opponent by sitting or lying on his back while he is prone.

body kinetics—the branch of biomechanics that deals with the actions of forces in producing or changing the motion of masses.

Brazilian Jiujitsu (BJJ)—a martial art and combat sport that focuses on grappling and especially groundfighting with the goal of gaining a dominant position and using joint-locks and chokeholds to force an opponent to submit or be knocked out depending on what submission method is used.

bridge—an escaping maneuver where one lifts one's hips and torso from the ground, by arching onto one's shoulders and driving with one's feet into the ground.

calf crush—a submission hold that causes pain from the application of force to the calf of the opponent.

cambo (Russian, acronym for *SAMozashchitya Bez Oruzhiya*)—the official martial art of Russia, originally recognized in 1938.

Chumakov, Ivgeny—author of *100 Lessons of Russian Sambo,* who is considered one of the forefathers in the proliferation of sambo, who studied directly with one of the creators of sambo, Anatoly Kharlampiev.

clinch game—a range of martial arts where one uses holds for standing control or dominance of the other opponent.

closed guard—a groundfighting position where one wraps and locks one's legs around the opponent.

combat physiology—the science of nervous, muscular, and hormonal arousal during human fighting.

combatives—the study of human combat tactics and techniques.

combat sambo—the non-wrestling martial art of Russia, used by the Russian military, police, and security forces. Combat sambo distinguishes itself from sport sambo—the international style of wrestling—and has become synonymous with mixed martial arts competitions, which began in Russia in the 1980s.

combat sambo Spetsnaz (popularly referred to as Systema)—the non-sport martial art of Russia, used by the Russian Special Forces (Spetsnaz). CSS distinguishes itself from combat sambo in that it cannot be used in competition of any kind since it involves tactics such as sentry elimination, bayonet fighting, and entrenching-tool throwing.

compression lock—any submission hold that causes pain from causing hyperflexion of a joint.

counter-technique—any martial art maneuver used to stop or neutralize an attack.

cross mount—(also cross-side mount) a groundfighting position where one holds the opponent to the ground by lying across at a perpendicular angle while the opponent is supine (belly up).

Dinamo (also "Dynamo")—the original sports and combat research center in the former Soviet Union where sambo was compiled, tested, and created.

E-F-G-H

elbow lock—any submission hold that causes pain to the elbow joint.

Fantastic Four heel hook—a submission hold that causes pain to the knee joint by twisting the heel in an arm triangle hold.

fast-wrestling—any martial art or wrestling sport where a limited time on the ground is permitted for securing a submission hold. Fast-wrestling is different from positional wrestling in that it does not seek to establish a dominant, controlling position before attempting to apply a submission hold.

Figure-4—any hold on an opponent's body part using a triangle with one's arms or legs.

FIAS—Federation Internationale Amateur de Sambo, or the International Amateur Sambo Federation, the international governing body for the sport of sambo wrestling.

fire pole—in ground fighting, the action of sliding down the opponent's leg in order to control his hips more effectively in the saddle position.

foot sword—the outside aspect of the foot from pinky toe to heel.

free-style—the Olympic style of wrestling recognized by FILA and the Olympic Games.

fulcrum—the support, or point of rest, on which a lever turns in moving a body.

guard—a groundfighting position where one control one's opponent's body by lying on one's back and using one's legs and arms for full access to manipulate the opponent and minimize his ability to attack.

gulesh (Azerbaijan)—the national martial art style of Azerbaijan.

half guard—a groundfighting position where one controls one's opponent by straddling one of the opponent's legs, while on one's back with the opponent above, belly to belly.

heel hook—a submission hold that causes pain to the knee joint through twisting the heel and stabilizing the knee.

hip throw—a takedown from a standing position where the hip is used as a fulcrum to lever an opponent to the ground

I-J-K-L

Intu-Flow—the first program that stimulated the discipline of "joint mobility" in exercise physiology, created by Scott Sonnon in 1996.

Jigoro, Kano—juijitsu expert; founder of judo.

jiujitsu—An art of weaponless self-defense developed in feudal Japan that uses throws, holds, and blows, and derives added power from the attacker's own weight and strength.

joint lock—a submission hold that causes pain to a bodily joint by extending its range beyond normal function.

judo—a method of defending oneself or fighting without the use of weapons, based on jujitsu but differing from it in banning dangerous throws and blows and stressing the athletic or sport element, created by Dr. Jigoro Kano.

Kadochnikov, Alexey—a Soviet officer who developed and taught a system of combat sambo Spetsnaz using theoretical mechanics.

khapsagay (also "khapsagai"; Mongolia)—the national martial art style of Mongolia.

Kharlampiev, Anatoly—one of the three original creators of sambo.

Kharlampievian style—the style of sambo by Anatoly Kharlampiev, which is most heavily influenced by the national wrestling styles of the former Soviet Union.

kinesiology—the science dealing with the inter-relationship of the physiological processes and anatomy of the human body with respect to movement.

Kito Ryu Jujitsu—a system of jujutsu that emphasized kata, or specifically rehearsed techniques, that have been preserved by the modern inheritors of the system. These techniques, generally performed in full armor or in formal robes resembling armor, are centered on throwing an opponent to the ground.

knee bar—a submission hold that causes pain by hyperextending the knee joint.

knee knot—a submission hold where one laces one's legs around both the opponent's legs.

knee pinch—a groundfighting position where one grips the opponent's legs between one's legs; typically a weak position, but used in fast-wrestling for quick submission attacks to the leg.

koch (Armenia)—the national martial art style of Armenia.

Koshiki-no-kata—also known as Kito-ryu no Kata. It consists of 21 techniques originally belonging to the Kito school of jujutsu. Jigoro Kano revised the techniques and incorporated them into a kata in order to preserve the historical source of judo. Although koshiki-no-kata is not often seen in the United States, it is still taught and practiced in Japan.

kulachni boi—the sport of hand-to-hand fighting in Russia, as opposed to Rukapashni Boi, which is the self-defense and combat format.

kurash (Uzbekistan)—the national martial art style of Uzbekistan.

kurtka—the official jacket uniform for the Russian martial art of sambo, and required uniform for sambo sport-wrestling.

lacing (of leg)—the act of winding one's legs around the opponent's.

leak leverage—when a submission hold does not have a solid three points of a lever; for example, if the fulcrum is weak, then the submission hold does not cause as much pain because the lever "leaks" force.

leg lace—a takedown technique in sambo by winding one's legs around the opponent's while standing.

leg lock—any submission hold to the opponent by causing pain to the joints of his legs.

leg shoot—a takedown technique approach in many wrestling styles, where one rapidly moves toward the opponent's lower body, while changing levels or squatting down.

leg sweep—a takedown technique using one's leg to kick out the opponent's legs; most effectively applied once one has unbalanced the opponent, sweeping out the leg with the least weight balanced on it and pulling the opponent over.

leg triangle—a holding method using both of one's legs, one shin in the knee pit of the other, to create a "figure-4" lace around the opponent's body part(s).

lower-half positional fighting—the groundfighting range of attacking the opponent's lower body to control his ability to escape or move by securing his hips, or lunar plexus.

lunar plexus—the anatomical polar opposite of the solar plexus located approximately between the hips of the body; often called the "hara" or "dantein" in martial arts.

M-N-O-P

Master of Sports—the highest athletic distinction awarded in the former Soviet Union, and the current Russian Ministry of Sport, requiring one to win a national championship in one's sport.

mixed martial arts (MMA)—a full contact combat sport that allows a wide variety of fighting techniques, from a mixture of martial arts traditions and non-traditions, to be used in competitions. The rules allow the use of striking and grappling techniques, both while standing and on the ground. Such competitions allow martial artist of different backgrounds to compete.

mount—a groundfighting position where one sits above a supine opponent controlling his solar plexus.

nidan—a judo term referring to a second-degree black belt.

NKVD (*Narodnyy Komissariat Vnutrennikh Del* , or People's Commissariat for Internal Affairs)—The leading secret police organization of the Soviet Union that was responsible for political repression during the Stalinist era.

no-holds-barred (NNHB) ighting—the original name given to mixed martial arts sports due to the minimal use of rules, but since phased-out due to the misleading and politically incorrect implication that no rules are used.

Q-R-S-T

reverse saddle—a groundfighting position where one applies a leg triangle to the opponent's leg while one's back faces the opponent's belly.

RMAX International—a global martial art community started by the author, Scott Sonnon, in 1996, involving thousands of teachers, trainers, and coaches.

rubber guard—a groundfighting strategy developed by jiujitsu pioneer Eddie Bravo using a methodical progression of highly precise guard micro-movements.

rukopashniy boi (Russian)—Russian hand-to-hand combat fighting in non-sport format, distinguishing itself from kulashni boi, which is sport hand-to-hand fighting.

saddle (and variants)—a groundfighting strategy developed by sambo pioneer, Scott Sonnon, using a methodical progression of lower-half positions to control and maintain dominance of the opponent.

sambo—Sambozashchitya Bez Oruzhiya, or "self-defense without weapons," is the Russian national wrestling style, hand-to-hand combat system, self-defense approach, and martial art, officially recognized in 1938.

scarf hold, or scarf position—a groundfighting position that controls the opponent, who is lying supine, by holding his head and arm "like a scarf" while lying on one's side ribs into the opponent's solar plexus.

self-defense sambo—a branch of Russian martial art dedicated to hostile subject control and civilian self-protection skills. Self-defense sambo distinguishes itself from sambo wrestling and combat sambo in that it has no competitive aspect; and distinguishes itself from combat sambo Spetsnaz in that it addresses the law enforcement and civilian needs of neutralizing an opponent when not in a military engagement.

shoulder lock—any submission hold that causes pain to the shoulder joint.

shrimp; shrimping—a groundfighting maneuver where one moves from one's back (supine) to one's side, by bringing one's knee to one's elbow; used to escape from being mounted to placing the opponent in one's guard position.

side mount—see cross-side mount.

side saddle—a groundfighting position where one laces a leg triangle on the opponent's leg with the knot of the "figure-4" to the outside of the opponent's leg.

sinew separation—any submission hold where traction (pulling apart) is first caused before hyper-extension, -flexion or -rotation. By separating the tissues, the joint capsule causes pain much faster.

sits bones—the two bones of the pelvis that make contact with your chair when sitting.

solar plexus—the anatomical network of nerves situated at the upper part of the abdomen, behind the stomach and in front of the aorta. It also serves as a secure point to pin an opponent's upper half to the ground in groundfighting.

special sambo—also known as combat sambo Spetsnaz, or Systema.

Spetsnaz—the Russian military special forces and special purpose police units.

spider guard—a groundfighting position using the legs while on one's back to attack the anatomical cavities of the opponent, such as placing both feet in the opponent's hip folds to control his hips.

Spiridonov, Viktor—one of the progenitors of Russian sambo, who originally created sambo as SAMOZ, short for "self-defense" (Samozashchitya.)

Spiridonovian style—the style of sambo by Viktor Spiridonov, which is most heavily influenced by the indigenous styles of Slavic martial arts

of pre-Soviet Russia known for its "softness" and efficiency. Due to Spiridonov's physical weakness, he developed an approach that used maximum leverage to counter an opponent's superior strengths.

Systema—"The System" in Russia, also known as special sambo or combat sambo Spetsnaz. There are many "Systemas" in Russia: Kadochnikov Systema, ROSS Systema, Ryabko Systema, etc.

System ROSS—an approach of special sambo developed by Distinguished Coach of Russia and Cossack Military General, Alexander Retuinskih, President of the Russian Martial Arts Federation.

Tenjin Shin'yo Ryu—a traditional school of jujutsu founded by Iso Mataemon Minamoto no Masatari in the 1830s. Once a very popular jujutsu system in Japan, among the famous students who studied the art were Kano Jigoro, whose modern art of judo was greatly inspired by the Tenjin Shin'yo-ryu, and Morihei Ueshiba, the founder of aikido.

tourniquet—a technical nuance in the groundfighting positions known as the saddles, where the leg triangle is tightened to restrict blood flow and increase one's control over the opponent's hips.

triangle point—a physics reference to the breach of stance integrity in bipedal creations, such as humans, where on a line between one's feet, any line which intersects that line at a perpendicular angle causes a breach in stance integrity. This is used to determine where to throw an opponent.

Trînta (Republic of Moldova)—the national martial art style of Moldova.

turtle—a groundfighting position where one remains prone with shins and elbows on the ground and head tucked "like a turtle."

Unlike what many think, the turtle position is very defensible since the vulnerable body parts are protected, including the neck.

twist—a submission hold to the spine causing pain by twisting the shoulders and hips in opposite directions.

U-Z

upper-half positional fighting—the groundfighting range of attacking the opponent's upper body to control his ability to escape or move by securing his chest, or solar plexus.